ENDOR

Megan's Heart is a fast-paced, well-written account of the ups and downs surrounding a young woman's struggle with a failing heart. The faith of the Moss family and God's divine interventions along the way changed the way I look at life, death, prayers, and miracles. Readers will find it inspiring and life-changing, too.
Jo Williamson, Ph.D., College Professor, Atlanta, Georgia

Megan's Heart is both heart-warming and challenging. This book is a must-read for this generation and the next.
Aletha Hinthorn, Director of Come to the Fire Conferences and author of 15 books, Leawood, Kansas

After I did the Easter Sunday interview, it was inspiring to follow the family blog and see the world-wide interest Megan's need for a heart would create. Her story is a captivating account of faith, family, and community.
Mark Schnyder, News Reporter for KMOV-TV/ Channel 4, St. Louis, Missouri

Sharon Bushey writes compassionately about Megan's emotional wait for a donor (the death of someone to give her life), because she was the recipient of corneas that gave her sight. This book is a compelling, true story of how donor awareness and donations can give many a second-chance at life.
Brian Scheller, Clinical Coordinator at Mid-America Transplant Services, St. Louis, Missouri

Megan's heart story is the sum of medical science and technology integrated with the unyielding faith of her family and community. This spiritual path of her return to health and life is inspiring. As a part of Megan's team of health care providers, I am thrilled that others can share the Moss family's journey of prayer and faith to healing.
I-wenWang, M..D., Ph.D./Megan's Transplant Surgeon at BJC Hospital, St. Louis, Missouri

Currently, Heart & Lung Transplant Surgeon at IU Health Methodist Hospital and Associate Professor of Clinical Surgery, Indiana University School of Medicine, Indianapolis, Indiana

How refreshing to read about Megan whose squeaky clean heart desired God's will more than life.
Beth Coppedge, Former Director of Titus Women's Ministries, Wilmore, Kentucky

Although my parents told me often about miracles in their generation, the reader will see in *Megan's Heart* how my generation participated in a never-to-be-forgotten miracle.
Josh Dampf, Former Student Body President of MidAmerica Nazarene University

Youth Co-Pastor at College Church of the Nazarene, Olathe, Kansas

When reading *Megan's Heart*, I could recall the palpable presence of faith, belief, and hope that were present with Megan's family in her hospital room. When you can actually feel something, there is no doubt as to whether or not it's true. I know Megan is alive for a greater reason, and perhaps spreading her story and message is one of those reasons.
Gina Wagner, R.N./56ICU, Barnes-Jewish-Christian Hospital, St. Louis, Missouri

Megan's Heart

A True Story of a Heart Transplant Miracle

Sharon L. Bushey

Come to the Fire Publishing
Kansas City, Missouri

Megan's Heart
Copyright © 2012 Come to the Fire Publishing
Published by Come to the Fire Publishing
PO Box 480052
Kansas City, MO 64148
cometothefire.org
All rights reserved.

Library of Congress Cataloging in Publication Data:
ISBN 978-0-9838316-4-8
Printed in the United States of America

10 9 8 7 6 5 4 3 2

Cover design by Nathan Johnson

Table of Contents

Acknowledgements

I thank my husband, Richard, for sharing the journey of writing this book. Because of his insistence, I was at the hospital on Megan's first night of the April 2010 faith journey. His daily phone calls kept me strong during the 25-day stay at Barnes Hospital. He was also a part of reading the first draft and encouraged me during the lengthy writing process.

I thank Wayne, Kathie, and Megan for their willingness to share their personal thoughts and emotions so the reader could more fully experience their journeys. I also thank them for checking the manuscript multiple times for factual accuracy.

I thank my friends, Luanne Bibbee and Bob and Sheri Poel, who volunteered to edit and give suggestions on each chapter as I wrote.

I thank the friends and family members who were a part of my email prayer group. My weekly email updates not only kept the prayer partners aware of specific writing needs, but their responses kept me encouraged and accountable.

I thank Aletha Hinthorn for having the vision to accept this manuscript for publication. I thank Jeanette Littleton for using her editing skills to transform the lengthy manuscript into a publishable book size. I thank Nathan Johnson, Megan's husband, for designing the cover. I thank Gregg Hinthorn for sharing his publishing knowledge.

I thank God for allowing me to walk this journey with Megan, and then write about it!

Preface

Megan Moss, my 23-year-old niece, was admitted to the Barnes Hospital ICU on April 1, 2010, and on that day God began the most challenging faith journey of our families' lives. I drove to St. Louis to support my brother that night and lived in waiting rooms for the next 25 days. Early into the hospital stay, I documented the details of each blessing and miracle so we could transfer faith to our children and grandchildren, a commitment the women of our family made when we attended the Come to the Fire conference in November 2009.

I soon realized my spiral notebook contained only a fraction of the story.

Megan's story was told by St. Louis television stations and became available worldwide through the Internet. My brother's blog gathered followers from different countries as it chronicled prayer needs and God's answers. Family members and friends communicated by Facebook, text messaging, and the hospital's guest email service. All of these sources logged the story and timing of God at work.

Although I was an eye-witness and could have written a first-person account, I chose to write from a narrator's perspective. Hopefully in this format, the reader will see beyond the chronological events and experience the struggles and surrender that come with faith.

Join me now as we walk this journey with Megan, her family, her friends, and her God.

"Let this be recorded for future generations,
so that a people not yet born will praise the
LORD" (Psalm 102:18).

Chapter 1

Day of Darkness

* * * * *

Twenty-three-year-old Megan rested on the leather couch that had become her daybed since her diagnosis of severe congestive heart failure and hospitalization in December.

Unlike other days, the strength she often felt with daylight dissipated quickly. No matter how much Megan tried, she couldn't readjust her frail body where the seams of the cushions pressed against her thinning thighs. Her name had been on the heart transplant list since her recent hospital stay in early February, but weeks later she still waited and prayed, *Oh, God, please hurry.*

This wasn't just any Thursday; it was Maundy Thursday, the *day of darkness* some people observe as they prepare their hearts for Good Friday and Easter Sunday.

This Thursday was the darkest day Megan had ever known. She'd awakened thinking, *It will be another day like all the others: rest on the couch, listen to the juicer as mom concocts some nutritional drink, chat with the home-care nurse, take a nap, and hope for the phone call stating, "We have a heart!"*

But that's not how it happened.

When Scott, the home-care nurse, arrived to take routine vitals and change the dressing on the IV line, he asked Megan, "How are you feeling?"

"I'm fine," Megan replied. She was afraid any negative word would send her back to the hospital, and she didn't want to go there again until a heart was ready.

Suddenly she vomited the nutritional drink that Mom had created that morning.

Scott knew Megan wasn't fine.

How could I have gotten so bad so quickly? Megan inwardly cried.

* * * * *

A few miles away from home, Megan's dad, Wayne, felt weary. His job as an elementary school principal at North County Christian School was busy enough without the added care of his beloved daughter, Megan, or Meg, as he liked to call her. As soon as his wife, Kathie, had returned home from grocery shopping that morning, he had left the house eager to celebrate spring break by restoring a house he'd purchased for resale. He welcomed the solitude as he hammered in rhythm to his worship CDs.

18

Then Kathie called.

"Do we have a donor heart?" he asked hopefully.

"Scott says Megan needs to go to the hospital," Kathie replied. "But they won't have a room ready for a few hours so why don't you wait until two o'clock to come home."

Wayne was disappointed but not surprised. Although March held some sunny days with the new norm of portable IV tubes and home healthcare, the past week had included harsher days: fluid build-up, food reappearing, difficulty breathing, and the reality that Meg needed a heart transplant as soon as possible.

* * * * *

After Kathie ended her call to Wayne, she made a mental list of everything she needed to do in the next three hours. First, she would call on Facebook friends to pray.

She wrote: "11:00 a.m. The home-care nurse found Megan very weak today and is sending her back to the hospital. She needs to gain strength so that if a heart becomes available, she will be strong enough for the surgery. We are praying for strength, healing, and a new heart. God is able!"

Despite her desire to just hold her daughter, Kathie succumbed to the need to be efficient.

"Mom, we need to wash my hair; I haven't felt up to it all week," Megan said.

Unfortunately, washing Megan's hair was no longer an easy task. She didn't have the strength to stand in the shower for that long, so she and Kathie had discovered doing the chore was easiest if

Megan stretched out on the counter with her head in the kitchen sink.

Megan sighed, wondering if this might be the last time in a long time that she'd feel the pleasure of warm running water flowing through her hair. While Kathie gently massaged her head, Megan realized the warm water was no longer soothing; it was a vivid reminder of how helpless she had become.

And with every minute, more strength left her. *How will I ever have strength to get down from here?* she wondered.

When the towel was snuggly wrapped around her head, Megan slid from the counter with her mom's help and walked the few steps to the family room. Megan gratefully slipped onto the comfortable couch. In weeks past, she had rested until she had enough strength to comb and dry her own hair, but today her moments of rest were not restoring her strength.

Kathie realized how weak Megan was and took the hair dryer into the family room. "Megan, can you sit up so I can dry your hair?" she asked.

"Mom, I really can't!" Megan whispered.

Kathie placed dry towels under Megan's head and looked into her daughter's ashen face. As she brushed and dried Megan's fine, blonde hair, she thought about the last four months. Megan had good days and bad days, ups and downs that kept the roller coaster ride a daily surprise.

But this morning Megan seemed stronger, Kathie thought, even as her hopes of a good Easter weekend with family were vanishing.

With the last strand of Meg's hair pulled into a ponytail, Kathie stood abruptly and told herself, *I refuse to be discouraged. The hospital staff will help her have a better day tomorrow.*

Kathie headed to the bathroom to put away the blow dryer and damp towels. Next on the list was packing Megan's travel bag.

"Hold on to me, Megs, and I'll help you to your room," Kathie encouraged.

As soon as the bed was near enough, Megan fell into it.

I don't care what I look like, or who sees me. I just need to get to the hospital, she realized. As Kathie chose necessities, Megan thought, *I know I won't be coming home this time...unless I get a new heart. I have never felt this weak before.*

Kathie set Megan's travel bag by the door and scurried through the house to pack things she would need. The hospital was only 35 minutes away, but she'd learned from experience to pack for the long haul. She'd need changes of clothes, cosmetics, and a neck pillow for napping between interruptions. She definitely needed her laptop and power cord; they went everywhere with her since she used her computer to do scheduling for a telecommunications company. She'd take a good book. And, she needed some very dark chocolate for herself, and a few snacks for Wayne. She was ready...or at least as ready as she could be for whatever lay ahead this time.

* * * * *

Wayne couldn't concentrate on his work, so at noon he gathered his tools and drove home. He found his Meg in her room leaning over a bucket.

"I love you, Meg. We're almost ready," Dad said as he choked back tears and tried to appear strong.

Wayne and Kathie hurried to finish preparations. Finally Kathie went to Megan's room to get her while Wayne loaded the car.

"Megs, it's time to go," Kathie said.

Megan tried to sit up and scoot her feet off her bed.

"Mom, I don't think I can move," she whispered.

"Wayne, I need your help," Kathie called. Wayne dashed into the room and each took one of Megan's arms, gently lifting her to a standing position. Wayne and Kathie supported their daughter as the three slowly walked down the short hall to the family room.

"I can't do this. I can't walk," Megan admitted as her legs collapsed.

Wayne gently scooped Meg's frail body into his strong arms and carried her to the car. As Wayne returned to lock the red front door, Kathie tucked a pillow behind Megan's head and a warm blanket around her.

Only four months ago she was the supervisor of the front office at the Ritz-Carlton, and today she can't even walk, Kathie thought. *Oh, God, help us through this dark day.*

* * * * *

Wayne and Kathie had learned that two cars were necessary for their hospital visits: one for the caregiver who stayed at the hospital, and one for the parent who returned home for a few hours of sleep. Wayne hurried ahead hoping to find a parking space in the hospital garage, secure a wheelchair, and be waiting at the roadside drop-off when Megan arrived.

I wonder when I last carried her, he thought, as he drove down the street. *Perhaps she was seven or eight.* Too old to be carried, he was sure.

Meg had fallen asleep on the way home from church—or pretended to be asleep—so she could enjoy one more of those "safe-in-Daddy's-arms" trips to bed. He hadn't cared that she was faking; he'd savored the moment since his baby girl was growing so fast.

Wayne's van passed his mom and dad's house. He had grown up here in Ferguson, Missouri, a suburb of St. Louis, in the comfort of home, church, and community. Then he'd married his college sweetheart and brought her back to Ferguson. His jobs as a youth pastor, associate pastor, and Christian school administrator had taken them to Oklahoma, Michigan, and Texas—but then they returned to Ferguson to live only a few miles from where his life began.

So much had changed in the family mosaic the past few years. His oldest daughter, Mandi, had been married to Kyle for almost five years when the birth of Kinsley made him a grandpa.

Next his mind shifted to 21-year-old Jason. *Hard to believe he's married.* He could still picture the beautiful outdoor wedding Jason and his wife, Dani, had months earlier—unfortunately, on about the coldest October day in St. Louis history!

Less than six months ago I was dancing with my beautiful Meg, as close to the column heaters as we could get. He knew she had hoped to be married before her younger brother, but that night she'd seemed content to let her daddy be her man. *I'm so glad, Lord, that she has been willing to wait for your best...Oh, God, please spare my baby girl's life so she can have a wedding some day.*

As Wayne neared the hospital, he called his sisters. Sheryl lived near his mom and dad and could break the news to them. He then called his oldest sister, Sharon, who lived a few hours away and his youngest sister, Shar, in California.

As the too-familiar buildings of the Barnes-Jewish-Christian Hospital complex came into view, Wayne prayed, *Lord, you know how sick Megan is and how every minute counts. Please help me find a parking space and a wheelchair.*

He turned into the parking garage across the street from the hospital hoping to find a space near the entrance. There it was: a parking space with an abandoned wheelchair next to it.

Thank you, Lord. You care about even the little details of our lives!

Wayne wasn't a sprinter, but today his personal training came in handy. Running with the wheelchair through the garage and across the street, he was at the curbside drop-off just as Kathie and Megan arrived.

Wayne helped Megan into the wheelchair. As Kathie and Megan hurried to the in-patient registration desk, Wayne jumped behind the wheel of Kathie's car and took it to the parking garage.

When Wayne arrived, he saw Megan throw up and Kathie gently wipe Meg's mouth. He knew the admitting process could take 45 minutes or more as they signed papers and waited for transport. He was relieved when the admitting clerk ignored procedure and personally took Megan to her second-floor room.

Wayne and Kathie were surprised they hadn't been assigned to the eighth floor cardiac unit where Megan had stayed before, but at least Megan had a bed. The second-floor medical staff repeatedly entered and exited the room without conversing.

"What is going on?" Kathie asked Wayne. "Can't they see how sick Meg is? Why aren't they doing anything besides checking her?"

While Wayne and Kathie waited *not* so patiently for nurses and doctors to begin Megan's care, Wayne called their pastor and requested, "Please begin the prayer chain."

Wayne finally asked the nurse about their plan for Meg's care.

"Megan's condition is too critical for this unit," the nurse explained. "We're preparing to move her into the Cardiac Intensive Care Unit."

This was more serious than their previous visits to the cardiac unit. Wayne and Kathie hugged each other. During Megan's two previous hospital stays, they had watched three Cardiac ICU families grieve the loss of their loved ones in that unit.

Within minutes Megan was wheeled to the Cardiac Intensive Care Unit (also called CCU), and her intensive care began. Strong medications flowed through the IVs to increase Megan's heart function. As the staff surrounded Megan with equipment, wires, and tubes, Wayne retreated to the waiting room to update his praying friends on Facebook: "4:30 p.m. Meg is in the Cardiac Intensive Care Unit getting additional meds to help her heart beat strong enough to send blood to her vital organs. Thanks for the prayers."

On this dark day, Wayne and Kathie realized that all they could do was pray and wait.

Chapter 2

Christ Is Enough

Thursday, April 1

* * * * *

Sharon had almost finished preparing the music for the Maundy Thursday service when her brother Wayne called to tell her that Megan was on her way to the hospital. Although she agreed to pray, she also wanted to support her brother.

"Why not go be with him? This is one of the benefits of being the older, recently retired sister," she reasoned. With her husband, Richard's, encouragement, she spent the rest of the afternoon preparing for the possibility of a trip to St. Louis a couple of hours from her home in central Missouri.

As Sharon packed, she thought of Megan's desperate need for a donor. Sharon was thankful Megan's spiritual heart was disease-free, but because Megan's physical heart was failing, in order for Megan to live, she needed someone to die —someone whose family was willing to look beyond their own grief and loss to donate their loved one's heart.

Sharon wasn't prepared for Wayne's update when she called him on her way to church.

"They moved Megan to CCU, and her name is now at the top of the heart transplant list."

"I'm praying and will call you as soon as church is over," Sharon said.

Richard could see his wife's distress and said, "You don't have to stay, you know; you can leave now."

Sharon thanked Richard for his support and hurried to change her plans.

* * * * *

The buzzer sounded and the CCU doors opened. Room 8 on the right was Sharon's destination. On the visits in December, Sharon always found a bright-eyed, pleasant niece who showed no concern over her desperate situation.

Tonight Sharon didn't know what to expect.

She peeked beyond the curtain in the room and was surprised to see a picture of peace. In the midst of tubes, IV bags, and machines, Kathie, Wayne, and Megan were holding hands and praying.

"God, give Meg a good night's sleep," Wayne prayed. "We trust you with her life and her need for a heart. Be with the donor's family and give them peace."

Megan opened her eyes. She smiled and motioned for her Aunt Sharon to join them while Wayne continued. "We trust Meg into your care tonight. In Jesus' name we pray, Amen."

When Wayne opened his eyes, he was surprised to see his sister by his side. He hugged her and headed for home to get some sleep.

As soon as her daddy left the room, Megan started chatting with her Aunt Sharon, and with each sentence she seemed to gain strength. Her mom commented, "Megs, you haven't talked this much all day. Are you feeling better?"

The second IV medicine finally taking effect was probably the reason for her energy, but Megan tried to convince her mom that Aunt Sharon's arrival had helped her feel better.

The staff gave Kathie and Sharon permission to stay in Megan's room throughout the night, but neither was allowed to sleep. Since Megan wasn't sleepy, Kathie decided to talk about some scriptures that had given her strength during the last few months.

First, she described how she groaned when she realized Lamentations was the next book in her daily Bible reading.

"'What will I find in *that* book of the Bible to encourage me?' I wondered," she explained. "But I started to read it anyway and God used it to give me peace." She opened her Bible and read Lamentations 3:20-23 (NIV), "My soul is downcast within me. Yet this I call to mind and therefore I have hope: Because of the LORD's great love we are not consumed, for his compassions never fail. They are new every morning; great is your faithfulness."

Megan listened intently and then said, "In November before I got sick, I came across a phrase that stuck in my head and became my motto. Would you like to hear it, Aunt Sharon?"

"I'd love to," Sharon responded.

Megan said with passion, "Through this I demonstrate that Christ is enough—come what may."

She went on to explain that her friends were amazed at her strength. Megan believed that through her suffering and uncertain future, her friends had been able to see that knowing and trusting Jesus Christ was enough for this girl. He was her friend during lonely nights and her comfort when she was afraid. He had been, and would be, her protector and provider...no matter what she faced or how this experience ended.

Testimony time was not over. Megan asked if they could sing her favorite song, "Sanctuary." For thirty minutes, they led each other in one praise song after another. Then Megan shared her paraphrase of two of her favorite scriptures: Jeremiah 29:11-13—God's plans for us are for good *if* we seek Him wholeheartedly, and I Timothy 4:12 —even though we are young, our witness for Christ can be powerful.

Megan believed that even this critical moment was part of God's plan for her.

This was the close of an eventful Maundy Thursday, but the *service* around this bed was not one of darkness, but of praise.

Megan was ready to get much-needed sleep. Mom adjusted the pillow while her aunt tucked the thick, white blanket snuggly around her niece's thin face.

* * * * *

When Wayne entered his brick ranch home that dark Thursday evening, everything was just as they'd left it that afternoon. The soft brown fleece that had covered his baby was still draped across the couch. As he passed Meg's bedroom, he gazed at her bed wondering when she would return home.

Wayne assured himself that at least he could rest well tonight knowing that Meg was feeling some better and that Kathie, Sharon and the efficient staff at Barnes would care for his girl throughout the night. But sleep wouldn't come. His mind raced through all the events that had brought them to this place.

The journey had first started the last weekend of February 2002. Wayne's heart had swelled with pride as he'd watched his 15-year-old sophomore hustle down the court with her high school basketball team. Megan had also played volleyball earlier that year and was looking forward to soccer season. Meg was one energetic girl.

On March 4 soccer season finally arrived. While running laps Meg experienced some shortness of breath but didn't complain. A few days later, March 7, Meg arrived in her dad's office on the second floor of the elementary building, and Wayne noticed that Meg was struggling to breathe.

"What's going on?" he asked.

"I'm not sure, Dad. It's just hard to breathe."

Normally Wayne only called a doctor as a last resort, but this time he insisted that Megan get an appointment.

The next day the nurse practitioner gave Megan a typical check-up and ordered a chest x-ray.

"Megan, you're having an asthma attack," she decided. "Here is a prescription for an inhaler. Use it whenever you feel breathing distress."

On Monday morning Dad, Megan, and Jason went to school as normal. After putting the breakfast dishes in the dishwasher, Kathie went to her home office. She was in the middle of her normal tasks when the nurse from the doctor's office called.

"Mrs. Moss, since Megan was one of the last patients in our office on Friday, we didn't file her x-ray film," the nurse explained. "One of the doctors in our office saw Megan's chest x-ray and noticed some abnormalities he feels should be checked as soon as possible."

Kathie called Wayne, "The doctor said Meg's heart is enlarged, and she needs to see a pediatric cardiologist immediately."

Tuesday morning, another x-ray and echocardiogram showed that Megan had myocarditis, a viral infection of the heart. Megan was immediately taken to the intensive care where the doctor explained, "This type of virus can take a person within seven days if it's not treated immediately."

Wayne stood helplessly beside Megan's ICU bed wondering, *How can my athletic daughter be so healthy one day and so sick the next?*

Amid the shock, Wayne praised God that he had insisted on the doctor's appointment. And he added praises that Meg's x-ray film *just happened* to be left on the illuminator so the doctor saw it. Wayne believed this was providential. He would choose to praise God and trust Him for the healing Megan's heart needed.

By Thursday Megan felt better, but the doctors explained that the virus had severely damaged her left ventricle. Megan would be on heart medication for the rest of her life and would probably have heart issues in the future.

Megan and her parents determined to enjoy the present and trust God for the days ahead. Instead of living in fear, they decided that together they would chisel out a new norm as they thanked God for sparing Meg's life.

Megan graduated from North County Christian High School, went to college, and started a career with the Ritz-Carlton Hotel in Clayton. She took a lot of afternoon naps, but overall, led a normal life. The first few annual heart exams showed a strengthening of Megan's heart, but then tests showed her heart was weakening.

Finally in September and October of 2009, Megan's heart was doing so poorly that her naps increased. Wayne often asked Meg, "Are you all right?"

"I'm fine, Dad," she always replied.

Now Megan was in the hospital. As Wayne tried again to sleep, he thought, *Surely God will provide a donor heart soon...won't He?*

Chapter 3

When Sisters Pray

October 2009 through November 2009

* * * * *

"Megan, are you feeling okay today?" Megan's boss asked as they walked down the long, floral, carpeted hall of the Ritz-Carlton.

"I'm fine," Megan responded cheerfully.

Though he moved on, her boss wasn't convinced. Megan never slacked on her responsibilities, but lately she'd lost some of the bubble in her personality.

As Megan ascended the stairs, she stopped periodically to catch her breath. She remembered the spring of 2002.

I wonder if it's my heart? she mused. *It can't be! Maybe I'm just out of shape.*

After dinner that night, Megan found her exercise DVD. She stared at the cover, opened it, and then closed it. *I'm too exhausted to start exercising tonight,* she decided.

The next morning when Megan arrived at work in the upscale business district of St. Louis, the flight of stairs from the parking garage to the lobby seemed steeper. Megan had to lean against the railing and rest before she could enter the lobby. The short distance down the hall left her feeling as if she were on the last yards of a cross-country race.

"Why am I so winded? What is wrong with me?" she said.

Megan mentioned the subject of exercise at dinner that night. "Hey, Mom and Dad, how would you like to work out with me this evening?"

Wayne and Kathie agreed. It had been a long time since the three of them had exercised together. After the workout they were flushed and out of breath but had enjoyed getting the blood pumping again.

Megan resolved to exercise, but with every day, steps became more difficult to climb, and the long halls at the Ritz drained her strength.

During the next few weeks, Megan's parents noticed that she wasn't as energetic during their workouts. Meg assured them, "I'm fine," keeping the fluttering sensations in her chest a secret.

By the end of October, it was life as usual in the fast lane at the Moss house. In between their demanding jobs and fall activities at church, the family worked on remodeling their kitchen. Wayne and Kathie were so busy they didn't even notice that Megan had stopped insisting that they exercise each evening.

* * * * *

Not realizing the tiredness and heart palpitations Megan had been feeling, Kathie eagerly prepared for a few days away.

Now Kathie had her suitcase, neck pillow, laptop, and purse by the door. A quick note and she would be on her way: *Meg, take good care of Dad while I'm gone. There are leftovers in the fridge for tonight. Thanks for making the hotel arrangements. Love, Mom.*

Kathie looked forward to her annual fall get-away with the girls at the Come to the Fire conference. She was already anticipating the times of worship with nearly two-thousand other women who represented many generations, cultures, denominations, races, and walks of life...women who were joined together by the common goal of wanting to pour out their hearts and lives to find a closer walk with Jesus and feel the warmth of the Holy Spirit's fire in their lives.

Seven Moss relatives and three of their friends met in St. Louis so they could travel together to the conference in Nashville. It was Thursday and still part of Kathie's workweek so she sat in the front passenger seat to have room to type on her laptop. Kathie knew she would come home refreshed and challenged, but for now, it was going to be chat, laugh, and try to keep tapping those laptop keys.

These ladies were like ten giddy high school girls going to camp. The miles rolled by quickly as they told silly stories. Nashville came into view just as the sun was sliding behind a hill. The ten settled into their three hotel rooms, freshened up, and opted to get to the hosting church early for good seats rather than taking the time for a good meal.

During each session from Thursday evening through Saturday noon, the Spirit of God spoke individual messages to each of the ten through the different speakers, singers, and worship times. They praised God in song, cried in repentance, and rejoiced in lightened loads as they gained new insights for living the holy life.

Every moment was beyond the group's expectations and hopes, but the Friday evening speaker, Linda Seaman, was Kathie and Sharon's favorite. Sharon knew Linda from college days. Once Sharon was able to get her mind past dorm memories, she saw a seasoned woman of God who had successfully weathered the storms of life—including years as a missionary and as the wife of a denominational leader—because of her resolve to praise God and pass her faith to the next generation.

Linda's goal at this conference was obviously to inspire each woman to truly believe that God is faithful and He still performs miracles for His children; the key is for us to expect them, document them, and retell them so that God's name receives glory.

Linda read the biblical account from 1 Samuel 7:12 where Samuel set up a stone to remind him of God's help and blessing. He called the stone *Ebenezer*, which means *stone of help*. Linda then told some of her own miracle stories describing God's help and blessing during the times of want and pain.

When Linda finished the account of each miracle, she dropped a white stone into a large glass vase. As the new stone hit against the former stones, the ping that resonated throughout the sanctuary seemed to say, "Tell your children and grandchildren and great-grandchildren yet to be that God is faithful!"

While Linda spoke, Kathie decided she would buy a nice vase and some stones for herself and each of her three children. After Thanksgiving dinner, she would summarize Linda's message and ask her children to look for God at work in their lives. When they saw God's provision, protection, blessing, or loving discipline, they were to write a word or two and the date on a stone and place it in the jar. Then the next Thanksgiving, they would praise God as they poured out their stones and remembered all that God had done for them during the year.

Yes, that is what I will do, she thought.

* * * * *

The conversation in the van going north was far different than the silly stories told in the van going south. It had been another great conference, and the women's minds were busy processing all that they had learned.

How can we help our children and grandchildren know God like we do? How can we help them to know they can trust God with their lives? How can we save them from the heartaches of sin and challenge them to pursue the path of no regrets? How can we help them have a faith that believes in a God who can do the impossible?

These were difficult questions that could not only be pondered—they had to be acted upon. But how?

Sheryl, Wayne's sister and Kathie's sister-in-law, hadn't participated much in the conversation, but her mind was busy praying about all that she'd heard. She thought, *This will be just another good conference forgotten if we don't have a plan.*

A good-sized town came into view, and the ten decided to eat at Applebee's to celebrate the good weekend together.

By the time Sheryl found a parking space, she had a plan. "May we have some tables in the back corner?" she asked the hostess.

As soon as the ladies had placed their order, Sheryl explained her thoughts to all of them. "It is important that our children believe that God exists, but we can't be satisfied until God is our children's best friend. It isn't enough that our children believe Jesus was an important historical figure who was a great teacher and did a lot of good things; they must embrace Jesus as Savior. I would like for each of us to pray until we know our children and grandchildren have a personal relationship with God."

The ladies talked about how their own faith had been solidified through the miracles they'd witnessed during their growing up years. Their parents had expected, asked God for, and looked for miracles. As a result, the ladies had grown up seeing people healed before their eyes. They'd seen their grandfather who was robbed, beaten with a hammer and left for dead completely restored physically and mentally. They'd seen people healed from cancer and from addictions. They'd seen God work miracles in other areas of life, and they'd even seen a couple of children pronounced dead begin breathing again after prayer.

They realized that God used these miracles to help transfer their parents' faith to the next generation...to their generation.

"Have our children ever seen a real miracle, one that would cause them to never doubt God's love and power?" they asked.

The ten bowed their heads again and Sheryl led them in a prayer of commitment and petition. "God, we will pray faithfully until our children know you as we do... and, in this coming year, help each of our children to witness a miracle so powerful and so personal that he or she will never doubt your existence or your love."

As the ten wiped their tears with their napkins, they decided to start an email group to share prayer needs as well as God's awesome answers. These mothers and grandmothers were determined to transfer their faith to the next generation. They knew there would be some Ebenezer stones in their jars by this time next year.

Everyone settled into the van for the last four hours of the trip. The rest of the journey was quieter as each woman considered what her commitment might require.

Sharon's cell phone rang. Her daughter, Karen, was crying and described her desperate need for prayer. Sharon responded, "Karen, I'm in the van on the way home from Nashville. May I share your needs and ask the others to pray, too?"

"Of course!"

"Well, Come-to-the-Fire Sisters," Sharon said between her own tears, "we have our first assignment."

She told the ladies about Karen's prayer need, and someone near the center of the van began to pray so that everyone could hear.

Then the prayers changed to be about their other children. These ladies weren't just asking for handouts from a generous God; they were asking God for a miracle that would build faith in their children: one that would be so miraculous that God would get the credit. As they parted a while later, they had no idea how God would choose to show Himself to their children, but they knew He would. They suspected they'd have some awesome stories to share on their way to the next year's Come to the Fire conference.

Chapter 4

Written on Stones

November 2009 through March 30, 2010

* * * * *

True to her plan from the Come to the Fire
conference, a few weeks later, before everyone left
the Thanksgiving table, Kathie said, "I have
something special to give you."

With a vase in one hand and a bag of stones in
the other, she told about the life-changing Come to
the Fire conference she had attended. After
explaining the significance of the stones, she looked
into the faces of each of her children and said, "I
have been praying that God will show my
children's and grandchildren's generations that He
still performs miracles in His people's lives."

Kathie looked at her one-year-old
granddaughter, Kinsley, with her curly blonde hair
and said, "Someday I want Kinsley and my other
grandchildren to point to my jar of stones and say,
'Mimi, what are these stones for?' On that day I can

tell Kinsley and the others about all the miracles Mimi and Papa have seen God perform."

As Kathie handed Mandi, Megan, and Jason their vases and stones, she challenged them to watch for God to perform miracles and give them blessings in the coming year. She instructed them to write the date and a few key words on a stone each time they recognized God at work in their lives.

"Next year after Thanksgiving dinner, we will pour our stones out of the vases and recall God's goodness," she announced. She had no idea how God would bless their family, but she knew the vases would no longer be empty.

*****

Megan's parents were exhausted from the holiday and their kitchen remodeling project, so they headed to bed for a Sunday afternoon nap. Megan wanted a good nap, too; she pulled her covers back, fluffed her pillow, and climbed into bed. As soon as her body was horizontal, her airflow stopped and she struggled to breathe. She sat up. After several failed attempts to lie down, she piled her pillows high against her headboard, and fell asleep sitting up.

Later Megan's brother and sister, their spouses, and Kinsley arrived for their weekly Sunday night family time. As Megan walked from her bedroom, Mandi hugged her and said, "Meg, what's wrong with you? Your face looks bigger!"

Megan simply walked away. She sat quietly for most of the evening, not even playing with the niece she normally found to be irresistible. She wondered, *How long can I keep my secret?*

As soon as the kids headed home, Wayne headed for bed, knowing the next day would be busy.

Megan sat in the family room watching her mom empty the lower kitchen cupboards and drawers, making a mess as she prepared for a new kitchen countertop to be installed the next morning.

Kathie turned off the kitchen light and stopped by Megan's chair to kiss her goodnight.

"Mom, I think we need to make an appointment with the cardiologist," Megan announced.

"Oh, what's going on?" Kathie asked.

Megan explained her struggle to breathe over the last several weeks, noting how the situation had become more severe that day.

Kathie knew enough. She awakened Wayne and they agreed: Megan needed to go to the emergency room.

The ER doctor at St. John's Hospital admitted Megan with a diagnosis of severe congestive heart failure. Lasix immediately relieved some of Megan's symptoms, but she'd need several tests before a complete prognosis could be given.

Since it would be a while before Megan would get a room and hours before the test results were back, Wayne returned home. It was 2:00 a.m. and only a few hours until the alarm would sound.

The first thing on Wayne's Monday morning agenda was to go to school for his morning routine of praying with the teachers and supervising the student drop-off area. He let everyone at school know he would probably be gone for the rest of the day since Megan was in the hospital.

Next Wayne hurried home to let the countertop installers into the house. While they worked, he called family members to update them on Megan's hospitalization. Finally the men packed their tools, and Wayne followed them out the door.

When he got to the hospital, Wayne learned that Megan had lost six pounds of fluid, thanks to the Lasix, and was feeling much better. But then the cardiologist updated them on Megan's ejection fraction (EF) tests. The EF is the fraction of blood pumped out of the ventricles of the heart with each heartbeat. Healthy individuals have an EF of anywhere between 50 percent and 75 percent. He told them that Megan's last ejection fraction in October 2008 had been 36 percent; now her EF was only 10-13 percent.

Though Megan heard everything the doctor said, she thought that surely he was mistaken and her heart wasn't doing *that* poorly. *I feel so much better since taking the Lasix; surely I'm not really that sick,* Megan thought. She was glad that today was her regular day off, but she knew from her experience with hospitals that she probably wouldn't get to the Ritz the next day.

When the doctor left the room, Megan asked, "Mom, will you call Andrew and let him know I probably won't be there tomorrow. Actually, I'm kind of excited to take a sick day."

"This is the first time you've ever used a sick day at work, isn't it?" Kathie commented as she dialed the number.

When she got Megan's boss on the line, Kathie explained, "We had to take Megan to the ER last night. She was diagnosed with congestive heart failure, but she's much better now. She'll need to use a sick day tomorrow but plans to be back at work on Wednesday."

"Megan has congestive heart failure and she'll be back Wednesday?" Andrew asked with disbelief.

"Yes. She's doing much better, and she'll see you on Wednesday," Kathie insisted.

Suddenly Wayne thought about the mess he'd left at home. *Oh, no! We won't be able to take showers tonight until the water can be turned on. And that won't happen until we install the kitchen sink and faucets.*

Knowing Megan had more tests ahead before they would release her, Wayne realized it might be very late before they would get home and he could take care of the water issue.

After a moment of silent prayer, he decided to call his good friend, Todd. Todd quickly assured Wayne that he'd help so the water would be on that night.

Thank God for good friends! Wayne noted, not realizing just how much he'd depend on friends in the coming weeks.

Hours of tests revealed that not only was the doctor *not* being unduly pessimistic, but also Megan's heart could stop at any moment. The only choice was to surgically place a defibrillator above her heart to shock it back into action if it should stop. Realizing that Megan would eventually be a heart transplant candidate, the doctors decided the defibrillator surgery needed to be done at Barnes, the hospital where she would eventually need to be.

So instead of going home on Tuesday morning, Megan used her sick day to travel from St. John's to Barnes-Jewish-Christian Hospital, which they usually called Barnes, in downtown St. Louis.

At Barnes the medical staff described the surgery, the placement options, and the after-surgery procedures.

What will my scar look like? Megan wondered, her emotions a blur. *Which of my clothes can I wear without revealing my ugly scar? What will people think when they see this huge bump under my clothes?*

But regardless of what people might think, Megan learned surgery and a scar were not options; they were critical to her life.

The surgery to insert the defibrillator went well. During the days of recuperation in the hospital, Megan spent her spare moments making scripture cards to decorate her room. When family and friends visited, she got them to help her.

After two weeks in the hospital, Megan was finally going home. Since Megan had age and otherwise perfect health in her favor, the cardiac staff wanted to give her new heart medications time to work before placing her name on a transplant list.

The family was encouraged when the doctors told them that medication might make Megan's heart strong enough to go several more months, or even years, without a transplant.

"Because you never used tobacco, alcohol, or drugs, and have eaten a proper diet, you have a significantly higher chance of recovery than your peers," one of the doctors announced. "Congratulations, Megan, on choosing a healthy lifestyle!"

* * * * *

Life had been so crazy-busy that now it was only a few weeks until Christmas and Kathie hadn't even taken time to sort and file her notes and materials from the Come to the Fire conference in early November.

She approached her cleaning tasks that day with a resolve to be thorough. As she sorted her notes, she read and reread the scripture from Ezekiel 36:23 (NIV): "Then the nations will know that I am the LORD, declares the Sovereign LORD, when I show myself holy through *you* before their eyes."

Kathie believed that God was telling her that He would take Megan's heart story to the nations, but she questioned, "We hardly know anyone outside of the U.S. How will you take *this* to the *nations*?"

She had no answer for her question, but she knew she needed to remember this moment.

While Megan rested in the family room day after day, Kathie shopped and wrapped Christmas gifts. Wayne worked at the kitchen project. Megan watched as he meticulously planned a design for the stone tile. He explained that he wanted the back-splash to be a beautiful focal point and highlight Kathie's trendy faucet.

I have such good parents! Megan often thought as she observed them.

As Megan rested in December, her strength increased and she appeared to be getting back to normal. She enjoyed Christmas and a New Year's holiday with family, even going to several parties with her friends.

On January 3 the roller coaster ride began. Megan started regurgitating her food and became incredibly weak. She had lost six pounds since her hospital admission on November 30, but now she rapidly lost even more weight.

Five days later, her nausea appeared to be under control and Megan tried to go back to work. But she was not getting better. After another week of vomiting, Megan was back in Barnes Hospital.

Megan's doctors determined that her heart was not responding to the medications. On February 2, 2010, she was officially placed on the heart transplant list as a 1B status; she had more priority than those with a status of 2, but her need was not as critical as those listed as 1A. She was also given a permanent IV until a heart became available.

On February 6, she again rode the hospital wheelchair to the roadside pick-up where her dad and cousin Trevor helped her into the car. Although she was going home with a port and IV and would need home-care nurses to check her regularly, at least she was going home.

Megan had several good days and even enjoyed a few short shopping trips. She was glad she had an assortment of big purses so she could choose which bag would accessorize her outfit while camouflaging her IV equipment.

Every day Megan and her family wondered if this might be the day that they would get the call from Dr. Ewald, the cardiac transplant director, saying, "I have a heart. Meet me at the hospital as soon as possible."

* * * * *

In March the bad days were increasing. The frequent throwing up, odd pains, rapid weight loss, and weakness were all taking their toll on Megan and her parents. Megan now weighed 97 pounds but could gain five pounds overnight from fluid retention: the more the fluid retention, the greater the pain and shortness of breath.

The days were long and the nights even longer. *Waiting is such a difficult part of God's plan,* Megan thought.

Megan wrote in her journal: "I am so ready at this point for the next step: *The Call.* Lord, I feel like I am climbing a big mountain, and it is taking forever to get to the top. *The Call* that a heart is available will help me reach the mountaintop! It will give me new life. Then I can slide down the recovery side and soon get back to my adventures in life."

Megan's bedroom was just across the hall from her parents', but her voice was so weak they knew they wouldn't hear her if she called. They moved the baby monitor from Kinsley's napping place into Meg's room so they could hear her throughout the night.

The calls during the night increased, and sleep eluded Megan more and more. Sometimes she was restless, but other times she became afraid as she contemplated the death of her own heart and the surgery that would give her a new heart.

She also spent many hours thinking about the donor. *Is he or she a Christian and ready to die?*

As she wiped her tears in the dark, she prayed for the donor and the donor's family.

One night as sleep wouldn't come, Megan realized that the same Jesus she had asked to come into her heart when she was a little girl was willing to be her best friend. *Mom and Dad are in the next room, but Jesus is right here with me.* She was overwhelmed with excitement when she grasped this wonderful truth in a new way.

One night she was especially jittery from the medications, and fear was hovering close. She spoke aloud to her best friend, "Jesus, please hold me as I sleep tonight and help me not to be afraid." Immediately Megan felt a presence beside her; the jittery muscles calmed, and she fell soundly asleep, feeling as if she were being held in the arms of Jesus.

Another night when Megan's mind raced, she reached for her journal and wrote: *God, I know You have a plan for me. You said it will prosper me and not harm me; it will give me a hope and a future. Father, I am ready. I am willing. I am listening. Please soften me so You can mold me into the woman You want me to be. I want to be a living example for You. I know you have something in store for me. I pray I am ready to handle whatever it is.*

With a calm smile, Megan wrote the final words: *I am excited and honored You have chosen to use me. Come what may, I love you with my whole, yet weakening, heart. In your precious name, I pray. Amen.*

Megan forgot that the baby monitor was carrying her songs and prayers to her parents' room. Many nights Wayne and Kathie fell asleep hearing Megan's serenades of praise.

* * * * *

Megan's regular clinic appointment was scheduled for the first week of April, but Kathie was concerned about Megan's decline and rescheduled the appointment for Tuesday, March 30. Even though this was the first time Megan needed a wheelchair to get from the car to the office, she wanted to convince Dr. Ewald that she only needed a little nutrition so she wouldn't be hospitalized yet.

In the examining room, Megan's next task was to climb up on the table and look *normal*. It didn't work. The nurses saw an extremely weak girl whose congestive heart condition was causing her to starve to death and announced, "She needs to be admitted to the hospital!"

Megan just tried to sit straighter and smile more intently.

"Megan, how are you doing today?" the doctor asked as he entered the room.

Megan answered in a forced, chipper tone, "Fine, thank you. Dr. Ewald, I will be okay if I can just get some nutrition. Since I already have a 24-hour IV with two lines, could I just have another one for nutrition?"

"No, we can't do that," Dr. Ewald responded. "A nutritional line would increase the chance of infection."

Megan heard only the word, "No" and became nervous. She expected him to admit her to the hospital. *If I'm admitted, I won't get to go home again...ever...unless I get a heart!*

Mom promised Dr. Ewald that she would keep trying nutritional drinks until she found something Megan could tolerate. The doctor agreed to let Megan go home for a few more days.

Megan thanked God that she was going home. But as she used all of her energy reserves to get in the car, she thought, *I am on my last leg.*

Wednesday was even worse, and the new drink didn't stay down. Megan had never been so sick in her life!

Chapter 5

Worth More than Life

Late Thursday Night, April 1 – Friday, April 2

* * * * *

Megan fell asleep as soon as her mom turned off the light in her hospital room, but the interruptions throughout the night reminded Kathie that her daughter was not well. Multiple blood draws. In-bed x-rays. Vitals. The checks seemed endless.

Megan's heart pounded at a high rate and the beeping monitors seemed to say to Kathie, *"I need a heart and need it soon...I need a heart and need it soon..."*

Even though the no-sleep rule was strictly enforced for CCU visitors, Kathie and Sharon wanted to be near Megan more than they wanted sleep. Kathie occasionally read her book by the beam of light from the hall, but mostly the two whispered, analyzed the monitor numbers, and concentrated on staying awake.

During morning rounds, Dr. Ravi indicated that Megan's stats weren't as good as he had hoped.

"I want to give the new medications a little more time," the doctor decided. "Hopefully they'll increase her heart function so her other body systems will remain stable as we wait for a heart."

Before leaving the room, he promised Kathie, "I will check on Megan often and will keep you updated."

While waiting for other specialists to arrive, Kathie jotted a note to her Facebook friends: "Compared to when we came to the hospital yesterday, Megan is *greatly* improved. After IV fluids and additional meds, Meg had Jell-o and apple juice and is feeling somewhat stronger. Pray that we will be able to 'bear witness' that knowing Christ is worth more than life."

After Dr. Ravi read the early morning lab reports, he returned to Megan's room. Megan appeared alert, but he explained, "Megan's kidney and liver functions are decreasing due to her weakening heart and inferior blood flow. If the stats worsen, we will have to insert an impella."

The doctor explained that the impella is a catheter-based assist device that is inserted into a vein in the left leg and unloads blood from the left ventricle. This device would reduce the workload on Megan's heart and hopefully increase cardiac output. With increased blood flow to the body, he hoped her kidney and liver functions would improve.

By the time Kathie finished talking with the doctors involved in Megan's care, it was nearing nine o'clock, the time when visitors had to vacate CCU. Knowing they couldn't re-enter until eleven, Kathie and Sharon headed to the cafeteria for a late breakfast.

Kathie didn't have much of an appetite, but the conversation was good for her soul. The women raised a lot of possibilities: God could provide a donor heart today; He could use the medicine to miraculously heal Meg's heart; He could prevent the impella procedure or could use the procedure for Meg's healing.

"No matter what happens, we just have to trust God," they agreed.

* * * * *

After Wayne's mind finally stopped racing, he slept well. When he called Kathie, she assured him that Meg hadn't had any significant change during the night. Since the temporary insurance deadline was nearing on the turn-around house, she encouraged him to spend the morning working. "If you relieve me by one o'clock, that will be soon enough."

When Wayne received the call the day before, he was gutting the bathroom. This morning he tried to continue this messy, multi-faceted project, but tears clouded his view. At 9:30 he gathered his tools and shut the lid on his toolbox.

I can't work on this house with Meg in CCU.

When Wayne exited the elevator, he saw Kathie working on her laptop.

"Why did you come so early?"

"I couldn't stop thinking about Meg," he said. He encouraged Sharon to go with Kathie to get rest, but his sister was determined not to leave him or Kathie alone. When Kathie disappeared behind the elevator door, Sharon leaned back in her waiting room chair to nap.

Since Wayne couldn't enter CCU for 30 minutes, he checked his Facebook and email accounts. Many friends had responded about Megan's admission to CCU and had promised to pray.

Wayne's phone rang. A friend who knew about the insurance deadline on the house was offering to finish gutting the bathroom, install the plumbing and drywall, change the doors, paint, and even lay ceramic tile in the bathroom and kitchen!

Incredible! As Wayne closed his phone, he thanked God with tears of relief and gratitude.

Finally, at 10:59 Wayne slipped his computer into his briefcase.

Megan smiled and hugged her daddy when he leaned over the bed. Wayne thought Meg appeared perkier than before. But soon she closed her eyes and slept.

"She seems stronger today," Wayne observed when Dr. Ravi entered the room.

"The IV meds help Megan feel better," the doctor explained. "But we're concerned about her declining liver and kidney functions. I ordered some medication adjustments, and we'll continue to monitor her stats."

Still Wayne felt some relief as he watched Megan sleep; she had slept so little during the last several weeks. *Maybe the quality sleep will restore her strength and promote healing.*

By mid-afternoon Megan's room became a flurry of activity: numerous blood samples, additional IV bags, multiple chest x-rays, and two echocardiograms.

Despite the rush, Megan slept soundly. She opened her eyes only when the medical staff spoke to her about a procedure and then promptly fell asleep again.

Mandi, Megan's sister, arrived late in the afternoon and asked, "Why is Meg sleeping with her eyes half open? Her eyes look at half mast!"

"I don't know. She's slept all day," Wayne replied.

Mandi approached a group of nurses in the hall and asked, "Why is my sister so unresponsive?"

The nurses jolted to attention at the word *unresponsive.* They ran into Megan's room shouting, "Megan! Megan!"

Megan woke with a start.

"Yes?" Megan said sleepily, looking at the people who were watching her.

She closed her eyes and went back to sleep.

The nurses said Megan had simply been in a deep sleep. But concern over Megan's extremely fast heart rate and excessive sleepiness prompted them to call her doctor.

"If Megan is losing liver and kidney function, does that mean she'll lose her priority place on the transplant list?" Mandi asked her dad.

When Dr. Ravi entered the room next, he confirmed their fears. If Megan's major organs continued to shut down, not only was her life in danger, but her name would also drop lower on the transplant list. The top of the list was reserved for relatively healthy people who had a good chance of survival.

* * * * *

After a brief nap and a hot shower, Kathie returned to CCU to discover that the only time Megan woke that afternoon was to get sick.

Throughout the evening, family members took turns staying with Megan while the others visited with friends who came to share snacks and hugs. Megan was oblivious to her visitors.

Unaware that the doctors were in a conference room frantically deciding how to save Megan's life, Wayne and Kathie said a goodnight prayer with sleeping Meg. Wayne told Kathie, "I'll go home to get some sleep if you're sure you and Sharon can handle it again tonight."

"We got naps this afternoon. We'll be fine," Kathie assured him.

As Wayne left, Sharon grabbed her novel and Kathie opened her computer to update her praying friends. "Amazing how things can change from morning to evening. Megs had lots of nausea; groggy, sleepy all day. God is still good. May I hear you say *all the time!*"

Kathie was still responding to emails when Dr. Ravi entered.

His shift should have been over hours ago...why is he still here? she wondered.

While he checked Megan, Kathie chatted. "She's slept a lot today; guess she's catching up on all the sleep she missed the last few weeks."

"Megan's heart is very bad," the doctor explained. "Sleeping is all her heart will let her do. Her liver and kidneys are shutting down. We'll have to do the impella procedure tonight. We'll start prepping Megan for the procedure shortly."

Kathie couldn't believe what she was hearing. "And, Wayne isn't here!" she said. Kathie called Wayne, Mandi, and Jason; Sharon called the rest of the family to put them on prayer alert.

* * * * *

Wayne had stopped to buy a gallon of milk on the way home from the hospital. Just as he stepped into the kitchen, his cell phone rang.

"Wayne, you need to come back to the hospital immediately," Kathie told him.

"Why? What's going on?" Wayne asked more calmly than he felt.

"They decided to do that impella procedure. Hurry."

Wayne tossed the milk into the refrigerator and headed out the still open door. When he finally reached the Barnes parking garage, he pulled into the first available spot and ran to the escalator. He sprinted up the moving escalator, down the bridge, and into the hospital foyer.

"Stop! You need a pass!" the receptionist shouted.

"I don't need one; I know where I'm going," Wayne hollered, still running.

A security guard tried to stop Wayne.

"My daughter is having an emergency heart procedure, and I have to get there," Wayne panted.

The guard waved him on.

Wayne arrived just as Megan was wheeled to the cath lab entrance. The staff paused long enough for Wayne to speak to his Meg.

Thank you, God! I made it in time, Wayne prayed silently as he walked with Kathie into the waiting room.

The attending physician, dressed in his surgical scrubs and cap, explained the procedure. "Once we get started, it should take only about 30 minutes. When we're done, I'll come give you an update."

As the doctor walked away, Kathie called out, "Remember, you are covered with prayer; we are praying that God will guide your hands and help you."

"Thank you," he said as he smiled and the automatic doors opened.

As the family waited helplessly, they realized Megan's body was so weak that any procedure was risky. So they did what their parents and grandparents had taught them to do: *Go to the Father.* They stood in a circle, held hands, and prayed.

Next Wayne called his Facebook friends to prayer: "Megan has gotten worse. They are doing a procedure to try to give her more time. We need a heart! *Pray!*"

Soon after the procedure began, a doctor entered the waiting room. He explained that during the last several months, Megan's veins had gotten smaller and weaker. The surgeon was having difficulty inserting the tube into the veins so the procedure would take a little longer than expected.

"Remember that we are praying for you," Kathie said.

Again, the group bowed their heads in prayer. They believed the Heavenly Father would work all things for Megan's good and *His* glory. They would choose to praise Him—come what may.

The clock ticked on. Midnight. 12:30 a.m. 1:00 a.m. Minds raced.

Are we really ready to bear witness that knowing Christ is worth more to us than life?

What is happening back there?

God, help us face whatever is Your will.

Near 1:30 a.m. the doctor returned.

"All went well," he said.

"Praise the Lord...and thank you, Doctor!" Kathie exclaimed. Megan's blood flow had doubled, but her parents were reminded that double of *very low* is still not good.

Kathie and Sharon returned to Megan's room, and Wayne reluctantly headed home, where he updated his friends: "2:10 a.m. Megan came through the procedure well. It doubled the blood flow from the heart. The next few hours are critical as they make sure the tube through her vein does not cut the blood flow to her leg. She is at the top of the transplant list; we need a heart ASAP. God will provide."

Wayne pushed the decorative pillows onto Kathie's side of the bed and folded the covers back only enough to cover his tired body. He was asleep almost before his head met his pillow; but the sweet sleep didn't last long. In his dream-state, nightmares began: Megan had died, and he saw his family and friends at her funeral.

He woke abruptly, realizing that the sobbing in his dream had been real; his pillow was soaked with tears. Relieved that it was only a nightmare, he tried to sleep once more.

Again and again throughout the night, Wayne experienced vivid nightmares and woke weeping. Each time he prayed himself back to sleep, pleading, "Please, heal my daughter. Oh, God, please heal her."

Chapter 6

The Countdown Begins

Saturday, April 3

* * * * *

When Megan returned to CCU from the cath lab, she was still sleeping off the anesthetic. Even though Megan wouldn't need them, Kathie and Sharon still wanted to be near her. After Megan was settled, they opened their novels.

Meanwhile, Megan's personal CCU nurse monitored the many beeps. She checked Megan's tubes, bags, and machines, entered data into the computer, and made many calls.

Kathie realized that if she was interpreting the numbers on the monitor correctly, Megan's heart rate that remained in the high 140s and her extremely low blood pressure were cause for concern. Sometime during those long, dark morning hours, the women were asked to leave the room. Kathie and Sharon stood in the hall and asked, "How should we pray?"

Kathie knew God *could* heal Megan's diseased heart. But *would* He? Was that His way of healing Meg?

After rehashing all the possibilities, the ladies once again came full circle: they would simply pray for God to do whatever would bring Him the most glory. They would pray Megan's motto, that through this, Megan would demonstrate that *Christ is enough — come what may!*

Not only is the hour before dawn the darkest, it is also the most difficult time to stay awake. Continuing her watch in Megan's CCU room, Kathie gave a Facebook update on Megan: "5:04 a.m. and Meg's been peacefully sleeping since 3 a.m. I see eleven IV bags. Sometimes it feels like this is not really real; that I will wake up and life will be *normal* again."

The early morning doctors' rounds confirmed the nurse's concern: the impella was not improving the blood flow enough, and the insufficient blood flow continued to compromise the kidney and liver functions. The doctor said he would make some medication adjustments.

At 9 a.m. Kathie and Sharon were reminded to leave Meg's room. As they relaxed in the cafeteria, a whirl of activity surrounded Megan. Besides her in-bed bath, there were blood tests, x-rays, and more doctors checking Megan's machines and stats.

* * * * *

Wayne was surprised he woke so early that morning. As he showered and dressed, he thought, *I need to get to the hospital.* He called Kathie to get a report.

She filled him in and added, "Don't worry about hurrying. Why don't you just come in at one?"

Relieved to hear that Meg seemed stable, Wayne thought about his plans for the day: first a haircut, next check on the house he was remodeling, and then drop by the bank. He'd get to the hospital by noon and take lunch to Kathie and Sharon.

Although the time clock was ticking on his turn-around house, Megan's time clock was ticking louder. His faith still believed for a miracle, but his heart nearly pounded out of him as he thought of all Megan had been through—and what their futures could hold.

The more he thought of her sweet spirit and sound faith, the more he cried. He wanted God's will for Megan's life, but his human heart couldn't bear the pain if God should choose not to heal Megan's earthly heart.

No more workouts together. No more after dinner runs in the neighborhood. No more hugs from his beautiful princess.

If that was God's will, would he ever enjoy life again?

After crying and praying, he begged God to give him strength.

"Your will be done, Father!" he said with agonizing surrender.

As he climbed in his van, Wayne sensed God saying, "Go to the hospital."

"Why, Lord?" he asked. "I really need a hair cut!"

As Wayne started to turn towards Great Clips, God spoke again, "Turn left!"

Since no cars were coming, Wayne turned around in the middle of the road.

* * * * *

Near the eleven o'clock CCU reentry time, some friends—Tom, Val, and Cathy—arrived in the waiting room with bagels and juice. Only four years earlier Tom and Val's daughter, Angie, had been diagnosed with leukemia. Her healing came only after a traumatic year in and out of St. Louis Children's Hospital. When Tom and Val said, "We understand what you're going through!" Kathie knew they felt her pain.

A team of doctors interrupted the waiting room conversation. "Mrs. Moss, we'd like to speak with you. And all of you may come," they added to the friends.

Kathie knew this couldn't be good news. *Wayne's not here! Why did we decide on one o'clock?*

She immediately called Wayne but his phone rang and rang.

Lord, you know I need him right now! And he'd want to be here!"

Because Wayne had obeyed God's command, he walked from the elevator with his ringing phone in hand.

Kathie took Wayne's hand, and they followed the doctors into a nearby consultation room. Wayne and Kathie sat on the love-seat with their eyes fixed on the four solemn doctors.

"Megan was alert earlier today, but then her condition deteriorated rapidly," one began.

Another doctor continued, "The impella procedure did not give us the blood flow we needed. Her vital organs are shutting down."

The doctors explained how very sick Megan had become. She needed an external left ventricle assistive device (LVAD) inserted. That afternoon.

"We hope she is well enough to make it through this open-heart surgery," he added.

The team tried to describe the surgery in laymen's terms, but the details were overwhelming. The listeners understood that this temporary form of a mechanical heart would help Megan's left ventricle function by routing her blood out of her body, through a large computerized pump at the foot of her bed, and then back into her body. This would hopefully buy her a few days as they waited for a donor heart. They also understood that if Megan did not receive a donor heart over the weekend, the doctors would consider putting a more permanent mechanical heart into her chest by the first of the week if she was strong enough.

Kathie felt sick as she envisioned her daughter's chest being split in two. She quickly turned her attention back to the questions Wayne was asking.

The doctors showed empathy, but this was a desperate, emergency situation and Megan could die during the surgery. However, without the LVAD, death was definitely eminent.

They also had another factor to consider, they explained. When the surgery ended, the countdown clock would begin. Megan would have a window of only a few days to receive a transplant.

Although the memory of his nightmares bombarded Wayne's mind, he consented to this major open-heart surgery. Kathie agreed; it seemed to be their only choice.

While the doctors prepared, the family and friends remained in the consultation room. They prayed, and then Kathie confidently quoted Lamentations 3:22-23. They would not be consumed by their grief, but their faithful God would see them through.

"Great is Your faithfulness!" she whispered.

Wayne texted a message to his kids: "Come quickly."

Sharon called other family members while Wayne and Kathie returned to Megan's room. Kathie insisted that Megan would want to sign the consent papers.

"I'm sorry; she's not aware enough to understand what she's signing," the doctor explained. "You'll have to do it."

With a huge lump in his throat and a shaking hand, Wayne signed the papers that would start the countdown. Now God only had a few days to provide a donor heart and save Meg's life.

While Wayne and Kathie stood by Meg's wasting body and beeping machines, they prayed for God to send the perfect heart so this surgery wouldn't be necessary. They prayed for Him to heal her heart and amaze the doctors. Then in submission they prayed, "But, God, we want Your will and want You to be glorified in this...no matter what! Knowing Christ is enough means more to us than life."

When the family left Megan's room so she could be prepped for the operation, Kathie couldn't get past the picture of her beautiful daughter's chest bone being broken, and Wayne couldn't stop rehearsing his secret nightmares and time of surrender that morning.

When Mandi, Jason, and Dani arrived, Wayne explained the need for surgery.

"I'm sorry to interrupt," a nurse said. "The operating staff will be taking Megan soon."

The family entered CCU, and Megan opened her eyes.

"Meg, are you afraid?" Mom asked.

"No. I have a calm all over me," Megan replied sweetly.

Time was short for them to speak what might be their last words to Megan. Mandi spoke first, then Jason, and then Dad. Finally Mom leaned over Megan's listless body, kissed her, and tearfully said, "I love you!"

Megan opened her eyes and softly responded, "Thanks for all you've done."

Kathie maintained her composure, but Meg's simple words seemed so final, so much like quotable *last* words.

When the orderlies whisked Megan out of sight, Kathie's composure that had been so strong for months broke completely. She fell to her knees and sobbed. Wayne and Mandi dropped beside her.

The three cried, as Jason walked up behind them, patting each on the back.

Megan's nurse entered the room, encircled the four with her arms, and cried with the family. Megan's prognosis was not good; there was a high bleeding risk since they hadn't had time to wean Megan from blood thinners.

At about 2:00 p.m. the family gathered their laptops, snacks, and other belongings to trek to the adjoining building—the waiting room in 56ICU—where Megan would be taken if she survived the LVAD surgery.

* * * * *

The next day would be Easter Sunday. While they waited for news from the operating room, everyone discussed "if" and "where" to go to church the next day.

The waiting room phone rang. Megan bled a lot but had made it through the surgery.

"Praise the Lord! She is still alive!" the family exclaimed as they grabbed their cell phones. Within moments, they were spreading the good news and asking for prayer regarding the bleeding. The message was passed from state to state, and church prayer chains began humming.

Sharon's phone rang.

"Mom, I couldn't wait to tell you what Garrett said when I told him that Megan made it through the surgery," her daughter Karen exclaimed.

With a lot of excitement seven-year-old Garrett had said, "Mom, I know why Megan is still alive. It's because I prayed!"

Sharon thought about the prayer of the ten women in Applebee's. God was answering their prayers: faith was successfully being passed to the next generation.

The surgeon entered the waiting room with the report that Megan came through the surgery as well as could be expected.

"If we don't have a donor heart by Wednesday, we'll do the surgery for the permanent form of the LVAD—if she is strong enough," he added.

The surgeon then explained that Megan would be kept in a chemically induced sleep for two to three days.

"Get caught up on your sleep while she's sleeping," he urged, "because she'll need you when she wakes up!"

The family was glad Megan's encounter with pain would be delayed, but it was difficult to know that Megan was literally being kept alive by machines: the LVAD pumping her blood and the respirator doing the work of her lungs.

Wayne and Kathie respected the doctor's professional plan, but they still chose to believe for a miracle before Wednesday: the healing of Megan's own heart or a donor heart received in time.

Although a mechanical heart would extend Megan's life, they didn't want their daughter to have this option for many reasons. The burden: having to carry an eight-pound battery pack with her for the rest of her life. The confinement: having to plug herself into a wall outlet whenever she was at home. The trauma: having to stay with friends or relatives if their neighborhood lost power, which had happened twice for as long as ten days in recent years. The unromantic inconvenience: these parents knew their daughter wanted to be a bride someday, and they didn't want a battery pack to interfere with the joys of a wedding and marriage.

"Please, God," they prayed. "Don't let it be the permanent LVAD."

Wayne was grateful for Facebook, the greatest prayer chain anyone could have ever invented. He wrote: "5:25 p.m. Megan's surgery went well. Blood flow is normal. She will be in an induced sleep for two days allowing the liver and kidneys to return to normal function. This will give us a few more days to find a heart. *God, Megan is in your hands now. We trust You with her and believe for a miracle.*"

Wayne took the night shift at the hospital so Kathie could sleep in her own bed.

Since Wayne would be so uncomfortable on the waiting room bench, his sister suggested that he take the sleeping bag in her car and bed down in his van. That way he'd get some sleep but would be near if he was needed.

Wayne complied and as he walked through the hospital foyer, he met his sister, Sheryl, with his other sister, Shar, her husband, Charlie, and their son, Grayeson, who had just arrived from California. After hugs and an update, he headed for his van.

Sharon was arranging her pillow and blanket on the chairs when Shar surprised her. While the adults visited sleeping Meg, Sharon played with six-month-old Grayeson and thought about this incredibly long day of unexpected happenings. It was difficult to believe that after Shar learned about the LVAD surgery at noon, she got plane tickets, packed, battled Los Angeles traffic, and arrived in St. Louis within ten hours. As Sharon kissed her nephew's forehead, she thanked God that whatever the family would face, they would face it together.

* * * * *

As soon as she arrived home, Kathie was eager to sleep but first wanted to update her Facebook friends: "9:22 p.m. Meg is sleeping like a princess. She is covered with God's love. Her kidneys have responded incredibly. Maybe tomorrow is the day —an Easter miracle? I think we're already walking in a miracle."

Chapter 7

Hope for an Easter Miracle

Sunday, April 4

* * * * *

Easter Sunday morning is supposed to be filled
with light and hope, but for Wayne the day began
with darkness and uncertainty. Instead of waking
early anticipating an inspiring Sunrise Service, he
woke abruptly, enveloped by the darkness of the
hospital parking garage.

He crawled from his warm sleeping bag into
the cold reality that his daughter was six hours
closer to the LVAD deadline. The countdown had
continued through the night, and he had not
received the call that a heart was available for his
dying daughter. He desperately needed hope.

"Megan did well throughout the night. All stats look good," a nurse announced as he walked into Megan's room.

The doctors later verified that Megan was responding well to the LVAD. All vital organs had responded well to the increased blood flow.

Wayne felt glimmers of hope beginning to surface.

Is God getting Meg's body strong enough to receive an Easter miracle...a new heart today? Wayne clung to this hopeful thought.

After eating breakfast with his sister, Wayne returned to his station by Meg's bed. He adjusted Sleeping Beauty's blankets and kissed her forehead, wishing his kiss could magically make his girl wake and be well. He surveyed Meg's seemingly lifeless body and many machines and then opened his notebook computer. He hoped his Facebook friends would read his post before they left for church. He wanted them to share the praise report and ask their churches to pray.

"8:00 a.m. Happy Easter. Meg had a good night; kidneys and liver are almost back to normal. We believe God is getting her ready for a new heart. I am thankful for science and God's gift of knowledge to Meg's physicians. The nurse said this technology was not available a few years back, and our baby would not have made it last night. We are living a miracle right now."

While the nurses changed Megan's dressings, Wayne talked with Sharon in the waiting room. Then Mark Schnyder, a reporter from Channel 4, KMOV-TV called. A friend of a friend of Megan's had called another friend who was the reporter's niece. This girl told her uncle that Megan Moss desperately needed a donor heart, and her family was praying for an Easter miracle.

The niece thought it sounded like a good community interest story, and Mark agreed. "If it works with your schedule, I would like to come to Barnes to interview you and your wife about 1:00 this afternoon."

Wayne had never been interviewed on TV and thought, *I couldn't do that*. But he said, "I'll discuss the possibility with my wife."

As though on cue, Kathie walked into the waiting room.

Before seeing Meg, Kathie wanted to hear about the morning reports. Wayne emphasized, "The nurses and doctors are extremely pleased with how well Meg is doing." He then told her about the possible television interview.

Kathie took a deep breath and said, "We shouldn't pass this opportunity to publicly praise the Lord."

Kathie remembered the scripture from the Come to the Fire conference and what she felt was God's promise to use Megan's suffering to *show His glory to the nations*. Would a television interview be one way God would accomplish His promise?

All morning Megan slept while more tests and x-rays were done. Meanwhile, her mom and dad arranged part of the cafeteria so the 25-plus family members could eat their Easter meal together. They also thought about what they would say with a KMOV-TV microphone in their faces.

"Isn't it amazing how one phone call can change your perspective?" Wayne asked Sharon.

"Instead of worrying about Megan, I'm sweating bullets trying to figure out what I'll say on television."

Since the reporter wanted the interview to take place with the family nearby, Wayne had to choose a place that would not only accommodate the food and family, but would be a good background for the interview.

As lunchtime grew closer, Wayne was concerned that the reporter and cameraman would arrive before the family and food. Wayne sighed with relief when he saw Sheryl's sons, Josh and Ryan, enter the cafeteria with food and a cooler. Sheryl and Don followed, carrying baskets of rolls and a cake. Within minutes the makeshift buffet table was spread with ham, sweet potatoes, veggies, and a strawberry-pretzel Jell-O salad.

In the middle of a noisy hospital cafeteria, the Moss family bowed their heads in prayer. They didn't know what they would face that day, and they didn't know the outcome of Megan's fight against time, but they felt assured that they were talking to the Father in heaven Who knew all.

When the KMOV staff arrived at the hospital, they first stopped in 56ICU where they interviewed Megan's surgeon. Dr. Wang told the television crew that they could take footage of the equipment but not of Megan since she had not given permission.

Dr. Wang briefly described Megan's plight and why the emergency surgery was necessary. Megan's condition continued to deteriorate, even though she was receiving maximum medical support.

The men thanked Dr. Wang and the ICU staff and headed for the cafeteria. Mark introduced himself and the cameraman to Wayne and Kathie. After expressing his concern for Megan's need, he explained the interview process and positioned Wayne and Kathie for the taping.

Although Mark asked about Megan's physical condition, the interview focused on the family's faith and their hope for an Easter miracle. When the interview ended, everyone breathed a sigh of relief and returned to their light-hearted conversations. Mark approached Wayne for one more off-the-camera question.

"Do you have this story written down?" he asked.

Wayne answered, "I have it on my Facebook page."

"Good! Then I have a suggestion," Mark replied. "When the news is aired tonight, we will have some viewers who will want to know how this turns out. You may want to build a blog site. Then we can put that link on our web page."

The blog would allow anyone to follow Megan's progress without having access to Wayne's personal information through Facebook.

Charlie and Kyle overheard the conversation and were eager to help Wayne with a blog site. So after lunch, Wayne and his helpers went to the computer in the 56ICU waiting room. Quickly, they loaded pictures and copied Facebook entries so readers could know the history of Meg's heart story. Wayne emailed Mark at Channel 4; viewers could access updates on Megan through www.megansheartstory.blogspot.com.

The afternoon passed quickly as the family visited. During one conversation, Kathie repeated the paraphrase of Psalm 22:3, "God inhabits the praise of his people," and reminded everyone that praise was a choice. During the difficult times as well as the encouraging times, she announced, no one was to speak a negative word in Meg's room.

"Understand?" she insisted with her winsome laugh and smile.

The family agreed, noting that praise and God's Word had always kept them secure in their faith during other trials.

Knowing he would probably be busy with people coming to see Megan and the family that evening, Wayne headed for his quiet corner in Meg's room to make his second blog entry.

• 6:00 p.m. X-ray shows extra fluid around her right lung. They're inserting another chest tube now to reduce the fluid. Still believing for an Easter miracle.

One special visitor that night was Erin, Megan's co-worker, who brought news from Megan's boss: a complimentary room was reserved for Wayne and Kathie at the hotel for as long as they needed it. They could see the Ritz from Megan's ICU window and knew that in an emergency, they could get to the hospital in just a few minutes. Megan's parents gratefully accepted this generous offer.

Another helpful act of love came through Jen—Mandi and Kyle's pastor's wife. Friends from their church, as well as Megan's church, had signed up to bring meals each evening. The family could access the *Take Them a Meal* site on the computer to know who was bringing dinner and even get a description of the food. Since Jason and Dani, Mandi and Kyle, and other family would come straight from work each night, there would always be enough food for at least 10 people. With a heartfelt hug, Mandi demonstrated what words couldn't express: *God and His people are so wonderful!*

By 9:30 most of the friends were gone, but many family members had remained to watch the ten o'clock news. The anchor introduced the top story for the night: "Family from Ferguson Looks for Easter Miracle."

"Easter Sunday for the Moss family was nothing like yours," the reporter announced. "Theirs was in a hospital cafeteria a few floors from where their loved one desperately waits for a new heart."

The next clips were of Wayne and Kathie who focused on Megan's faith. "She has been very strong through all of this and is confident that God will take care of her."

Wayne explained that on Saturday the situation had become a life and death matter, and that Megan was basically living on a machine, waiting for a desperately needed heart.

The reporter ended the interview with the words, "The Moss family leans on their faith this Easter as they pray that a life-saving heart makes it to Megan in time."

This was another somber reminder that what Megan really needed was a family who would want to give life when they faced death.

* * * * *

When Kathie and Wayne checked on Megan for the last time that night, the nurse reminded them, "Now is the time to sleep. Megan will need you when she wakes."

Neither wanted to leave the hospital, but they both knew the nurse was imparting words of wisdom. They needed quality rest while they could get it.

Kathie insisted that Wayne be the first to enjoy the luxurious room at the Ritz. "I slept in our comfy bed last night while you slept in the van. I got my rest, now you need to get yours," she insisted.

Soon a guilt-ridden husband left his wife and sister to sleep on the hard benches in Barnes while he slept in a plush bed at the Ritz.

Kathie and Sharon padded their benches with some quilts, but they needed to unwind before sleeping. While Sharon wrote in her journal, Kathie checked her Facebook account.

Kathie said, "Listen to this message that came from Shar's friend, Jo: 'Today the West United Methodist Conference family was here in Kennesaw, Georgia. They held Megan up in prayer in five services with probably about 3,000 attending. You are not alone!'"

Kathie and Sharon were awed by the fact that God was already taking Megan's need for a heart across state and denominational lines. He was in the process of showing His glory to the nations.

As Kathie put her laptop in her waiting room locker, she pondered, "You know, we didn't advertise that we have faith for a miracle. God did that."

Now *His* name was on the line and the community would watch to see if the God the Moss family served would answer their prayers.

* * * * *

As Wayne entered the Ritz-Carlton lobby to check in, several of Megan's co-workers wanted an update on Meg's condition.

What in the world am I doing in a hotel when my baby is so close to death? Wayne wondered. Nevertheless, he gratefully received his room.

Wayne knew his body and mind desperately needed rest, but as he lay enveloped by deluxe bedding, his guilt deepened. He cried out to God, "I feel so unworthy to be in this room; bless Kathie and Sharon and give them good rest. And, Lord, I feel so helpless as my daughter lies in a hospital bed hanging between life and death. Oh, God, how can this be happening?"

He cried and prayed in the privacy of the hotel room. He needed God to make him strong enough to face the unknowns of the coming week.

Chapter 8

What Is God Doing?

* * * * *

The family was only five days into the April faith journey when they realized God was doing something much greater than they could comprehend. Cards, e-mails, Facebook entries, and blog comments began coming in from all over the world—Italy, Afghanistan, Honduras, Africa, Japan, Spain, England, and more places.

Besides those who were already believers, many people considered or embraced faith as they read the blog updates. Surprisingly, other acquaintances and strangers sent skeptical notes or responses, even including blatant attacks against the family's faith.

Though it was rather unnerving to receive negative and even some hateful comments, Wayne and Kathie prayed for the blog and Facebook followers in all stages of faith as they continued to openly admit their desperation yet express their faith as they quoted the scriptures that brought strength for *their* days.

* * * * *

When Wayne got to the hospital on Monday morning, he was in time for the doctor's report. He and Kathie learned that due to the LVAD increasing blood flow, not only was color returning to Megan's thin, pale face, but her kidney and liver stats were also improving.

In spite of the good report, they realized the external LVAD was temporary. Within days, Megan would need either a donor heart or a mechanical heart (internal LVAD) would have to be surgically implanted.

With the good but grim news, the three began their daily routine. Kathie went to the Ritz to nap and shower while Wayne kept watch over Megan. Sharon got clean clothes from her car, used the guest shower, and returned to Megan's room.

When Sharon pulled the curtain back, her heart was simultaneously warmed and burdened. Meg's daddy was at her bedside with his open Bible. Not wanting to disturb Wayne's time in God's Word, Sharon slipped to the waiting room. The image of Wayne sitting by Meg caused her own heart to cry out to God: "Wayne is waiting to hear from You God! Speak peace to his heart. If you want Megan with You now, help Wayne to surrender. If You want Megan to be a *living* sanctuary, give Wayne a promise, give Megan a perfect heart, and give us all Your peace."

Sharon opened her own Bible and she stopped abruptly when she read Psalm 65:5: "You faithfully answer our prayers with awesome deeds, O God our savior."

She believed God would faithfully answer all the prayers for Megan, but she especially sensed that God was preparing the family for a faith journey like none they had taken. God would answer in *His* time and *His* way, and the answers would be awesome, not ordinary. God would answer in such a way that *His* name would receive *all* the glory.

* * * * *

The clock kept ticking with no indication that God was in the process of providing a heart. With heaviness in his soul, Wayne made the morning blog entry:

• 7:45 a.m. *God, I am pleading with You to send a heart for my baby. I know You are helping Meg do well on these machines, but she needs a heart or a healing of her heart. But, God, You know we have given her to You, and most of all we want Your will to be done.* "I will praise the LORD at all times" (Psalm 34:1). "The LORD is close to the brokenhearted; he rescues those whose spirits are crushed. The righteous person faces many troubles, but the LORD comes to the rescue each time" (Psalm 34:18-19).

Later that morning, a woman introduced herself to Wayne and Sharon.

86

"It sounds as if Megan might be getting an internal LVAD this week, so I'm here to describe the equipment and answer questions," she explained.

Wayne and Sharon listened again to all the details about cumbersome battery packs and inconvenient power cords. The technician also described the placement of the intricate mechanism that would take over the function of Megan's left ventricle.

Wayne and Sharon were more convinced than ever that this was not the surgery of choice for a vivacious 23-year-old. Although it would prolong her physical life, it would strictly inhibit her social life and would wear on her emotional well-being.

About mid-afternoon Megan's second drainage tube in her chest became clogged. The first tube had stopped flowing earlier, and now that the second tube was clogged and fluid was building around Megan's lungs, her breathing became more difficult.

A bedside procedure had to be done to insert another tube. When the process was complete, Wayne and Kathie were told that Megan's condition was still critical, but her vitals were stable.

* * * * *

Tuesday, April 6

It was barely 5:00 a.m. when Wayne woke and realized that the tiny love-seat in the consultation room was not big enough for his body; but he wouldn't complain. He was thankful that the nurse had offered this dark, warm room; at least he wasn't in the cold parking garage. Besides he was near Megan. He needed to stretch anyway so he thought, *I'll check on Megan before I get some more sleep.*

He entered her room and was surprised the nurse was lessening the sedation and beginning the process of waking Megan so soon.

The day before, when the doctor had explained the waking process, Wayne and Kathie were warned that Megan could hallucinate and be frightened when she came out from under the sedation. Wayne didn't want to go through this alone. He rushed to the waiting room and touched his sister's arm.

"The nurse is beginning to wake Meg," he said.

Sharon tossed her bedding in the corner and followed Wayne to Megan's bedside.

"We have to call, Kathie," Wayne said. "She'll want to be here." He added as an afterthought, "Mandi wanted to be here, too, but she wouldn't be able to find a sitter at this hour!"

Sharon asked David, the nurse, "Is it possible to stall the process until Megan's mom gets here?" He was willing.

The hotel phone on the nightstand rang. Kathie hoarsely answered, "Hello."

She heard Wayne say, "The nurse is beginning to awaken Meg. Come as quickly as you can, but drive safely."

While they waited for Kathie, David slowed the process but encouraged Wayne and Sharon to speak to Megan. When they exhausted their repertoire of things to say to a sleeping girl, they decided to sing Megan's favorite song, "Sanctuary," and then went from one praise chorus to another. David sang along with some of the worship songs, and then accessed a Christian music station through the computer.

As Kathie walked through the door, David decreased the sedation and told his helpers to begin asking Megan to squeeze their hands. He also told them she would probably instinctively reach for the respirator and try to pull it out; they needed to keep her hands away from it.

"And, don't let her talk," David insisted. "Talking will cause the respirator to hurt her throat."

As Wayne, Kathie, and Sharon called Megan's name, they watched for response. They followed the nurse's suggestion and gently explained the waking process, hoping to relieve Megan's fears as she re-entered consciousness. Repeatedly they told her, "Megan, squeeze our hands if you can hear us."

No response.

God, how long will this take? Will she hear us? Will she be okay when she does awake? O, Lord, help us! their hearts cried.

And then the squeeze came.

"Yes!"

"Thank You, Lord!"

Kathie, Wayne, and Sharon shouted with joy.

After several squeezes, the group decided to honor Mandi's promise to be with her sister when she woke. So they got Mandi on the phone, and she talked to Meg, asking her to squeeze Mom's hand if she heard her voice.

Megan opened her eyes and tried to speak. *Why is there a tube coming out of my mouth?* she thought and wanted to ask.

"Shh. Just squeeze our hands," Kathie directed. "You're not supposed to talk yet. It will hurt your throat."

For the forty-five minute wait before the respirator could be removed, Megan's breathing was monitored by a machine. During this time, Megan became frustrated. She had been in one position for several days and wanted to stretch, but every time she tried, someone grabbed her hand and said, "No, Megan, you can't pull the respirator out. It will come out soon. Just be patient."

Just be patient, she thought. *I can't talk; I can't let you know that I'm not trying to pull the respirator out. I just need to stretch my hand!*

Realizing that her family was going to follow the nurse's instructions, she decided to relax and hoped her breathing would improve quickly.

Shortly after the respirator was removed, Kathie remembered that it was her mom's birthday.

"Meg, let's call Nana to wish her 'Happy Birthday' and let Nana and Granddad know that you're awake."

With a slightly raspy voice, Megan whispered her first words, "Tell Nana...to tell me...to squeeze your hand..."

"Our Meg is back with us. Praise the Lord!" Wayne said. He composed a blog message to update the praying friends.

• 9:00 a.m. About 5 a.m. the nurse began to wake Megan. The process took a couple of hours, but by 7:20 she was breathing on her own, oxygen

90

levels were perfect, and she was communicating. God is *so good*! It is a relief to see her eyes and smile.

Although Megan was awake, she still experienced the side-effects of sedation. Technically, she had been asleep for two days, but her body was exhausted. Her tiredness kept driving her to fall asleep, but when she closed her eyes, horrors would fill her mind.

Megan saw monsters and people who wanted to harm her. At other times, she dreamed that she was alone—though she never was—or that her family, nurses, and friends were there but refused to assist her. In her dreams she would fall and not be able to get up, or the nurse would leave her calling for help. In one nightmare a heart became available but someone wrestled her to the ground so she couldn't get to the hospital in time to receive the heart.

Though Megan didn't go into detail about all of her nightmares, her family could tell she was distressed. To help her feel better, Wayne and Kathie took turns reading Facebook and email messages to Megan. One of her favorites was to Kathie from Megan's co-worker, Russ: "Sista, y'all got a gang of folks behind ya and Megaboo...can't nothing but good come out of this!"

Megan knew Russ was right. God's plans for her and her family were for good and not for evil—no matter what!

Later that afternoon while family members stood by Megan's bed, talking, she kept looking to her right, staring at the chair in the corner.

Megan finally caught Kathie's eye.

"Who *is* that?" she asked quietly, nodding toward the right.

"Who's who?" Kathie asked.

"The man in the chair," Megan insisted. "I don't think I know him."

By this time, Aunt Shar was also attuned to her niece's concerns.

"What man, Megs?" she asked. "There's not anyone here now except your mom and me."

"That man dressed in white," Megan explained. When they looked at her blankly, she pointed in frustration. "Right there!"

But suddenly the man was gone. Megan frowned.

"He was there," she exclaimed, looking at the bewildered faces around her. "But now he's gone. But he was there! There was really a man there! He was dressed in white."

Megan leaned back against the pillow and closed her eyes, twisting her eyebrows in confusion. *I know he was there! Whoever he was, I wish he would come back. I felt so peaceful with him there. He made me feel safe and comfortable.*

She opened her eyes again and looked at the chair. Now only Aunt Shar stood next to her bed.

"He was there," she whispered.

Aunt Shar smiled. "It must have been your guardian angel!" she announced.

What a cool thought! Meg decided.

Chapter 9

Blessings While We Wait

Wednesday, April 7

* * * * *

Wayne and Kathie couldn't believe what they heard.

"Because Megan is doing so well on the temporary LVAD, we have decided to put off the surgery for the internal LVAD until Monday," the doctor said with a smile. The unspoken words were, *"And we hope for a donor heart before then."*

"Why is Megan so nauseated and restless?" Kathie asked.

"These are common side effects of medication and Megan's worsening heart." He explained that he was focused on the efficiency of the LVAD, Megan's improved color, and the stable functioning of her vital organs. The doctor was encouraged, so Kathie chose to be encouraged, too.

In an effort to conserve Megan's strength, Wayne and Kathie restricted Megan's company that day. Wayne updated his blog, telling visitors not to come and asking for prayers that Megan would be able to eat. At the end of the day, he told his blog readers:

• 10:05 p.m. Megan's heart rate is still high (120s-130s) but she kept a milkshake, bowl of chicken noodle soup, and grapes down. PTL. She remained exhausted, but had a good day. *Thank you, Jesus, for this day, and we pray that Megan will be able to sleep through the night. Unless, of course, You want to wake us up with a heart.*

Kathie's post read:

• 10:16 p.m. Another sweet day with Megs. Sweet smiles, gentle spirit, funny thoughts, kind words. Encouraging words from the doctors. But always aware that she lives because of the LVAD and God's amazing grace. Thanks for your continued prayers.

* * * * *

Thursday, April 8

Wayne had been desperate for a hair cut since Saturday. Now Kathie needed a haircut, too. She called her beautician, another Mandi, and asked for an appointment.

"I don't want you to take the time to come to me; let me come to you. We'll find somewhere to cut your hair, and I'll cut Wayne's, too," Mandi offered.

Kathie was amazed by this gift of love. *I am overwhelmed, God, by Your blessings. Your people are taking such good care of us.*

When the beautician arrived, Kathie and Wayne claimed a bench in the park outside the parking garage where employees took their breaks. Kathie didn't care what the people passing by thought. Which of *them* had ever received a private haircut from a pregnant beautician while enjoying the sights and sounds of nature...and Kingshighway Boulevard? They were children of God receiving another blessing.

* * * * *

When Kathie and Wayne returned to ICU, Wayne wrote on his blog:

• 1:00 p.m. Megan slept better last night between three bouts of nausea. No vomiting though. They just lifted her out of bed and have her sitting in a chair called the shuttle. This amazing chair moves in all positions to help with muscle mass and bedsores. If you would like to send Meg a note, you can email her at www.barnesjewish.org. Highlight Visitors and Patients and then click email. They send your email on a nice card right to her room. Her room number is 56ICU, Room 1.

Later that afternoon, Wayne got a call from a number he didn't recognize. It was one of Meg's friends who wanted to do something special for Megan. She had called the manager of the former American Idol contestant, Danny Gokey, who had lost his own wife to a heart condition, and requested that he call her very ill friend.

Megan's friend exclaimed, "Danny Gokey's manager said Danny wants to talk to Megan. He would like your cell number so he can call you."

You're kidding, Wayne thought. *The Danny Gokey we watched on TV with Megan all season? The one we repeatedly voted for?*

Wayne was excited about a celebrity calling his daughter, but he was most amazed at how it had transpired. This friend didn't know that three weeks earlier, Wayne's sister, Shar, had also sent letters to Danny Gokey's offices requesting that he call Megan and "put a smile on a very sick girl's face."

Wayne found it amazing that Shar and one of Meg's friends had the same idea and contacted the same celebrity with the same request.

Danny Gokey called and the arrangements were made. He would call Wayne's cell phone at 1:30 the next day. Wayne told the family but gave them strict orders to not tell Megan. This was to be a special surprise for his girl.

* * * * *

Friday, April 9

"We have a surprise for you, Megan," her nurses announced. "We're moving you to a different room that has a beautiful view of Forest Park. It's much sunnier, and your family will have more room."

It was quite a process to make sure that all of the tubes and wires stayed connected to Megan and to the portable power source during transport. Two nurses claimed an assortment of IV bags and machines while two other nurses moved Megan's bed. The teamwork was incredible.

In the new room, a nurse asked, "Megan, what direction would you like your bed? Which view do you prefer?"

Megan chose to have her bed in the center of the room facing the two corner windows. *People in a five-star hotel would pay extra for this beautiful view,* she thought.

While three nurses arranged the equipment, the other one retrieved Megan's cards and decorative notes from Room #1 and displayed them in Room #12.

Kathie was overwhelmed again with God's goodness displayed through the nurses.

They could have put a new patient in here with a lot less hassle, she realized, *but they chose to bless us instead!*

Megan felt a little stronger and while she cautiously finished her liquid lunch, the family watched the clock anticipating Megan's second surprise. At 1:30 Wayne's cell phone rang. He touched the speaker button and said, "Megan, someone special wants to talk to you."

"Hello," she said.

"Megan, this is Danny," the confident voice rang out.

Danny who? I don't have any friends named Danny.

The conversation was a little awkward— although she recognized the voice, she couldn't put a face with it.

He finally said, "This is Danny Gokey."

Meg's smile widened.

Danny asked Megan about her heart condition, and she calmly answered. She told Danny how impressed she was with his voice and testimony during his American Idol debut the previous year. They chatted for fifteen minutes when the phone connection was lost.

When the phone rang again, Wayne answered and Danny immediately initiated conversation with him. He asked, "How are you getting through this?"

"It's our trust in God," Wayne explained.

"Are you a believer then?" Danny asked.

Wayne told him how Megan's and the family's faith had carried them through this difficult time. "Without faith, I don't know how we could have made it," Wayne said with conviction.

Danny assured Wayne of his prayers for Megan and the family. With a smile, Wayne passed the phone back to Megan.

When Megan finally said good-bye, she couldn't stop smiling. Her dad thought, *How neat that Danny Gokey, a busy musician, took the time to put a smile on my girl's face. "Thank you, Lord!"*

Now the secret could be told, and Wayne blogged:

• 3:00 p.m. Blessings outpour for Megan today: four nurses decided she needed a better view and moved her to a suite overlooking Forest Park. Best view in St. Louis. Then at 1:30 she got a call from Danny Gokey from American Idol. He encouraged her and lifted her spirits. Thank you, nurses and Danny, for being Jesus to Meg today.

* * * * *

Megan became restless during her late afternoon nap. Kathie looked at her daughter with concern. Almost as if on cue, a nurse walked in, glancing at her stats. She looked again. Megan's heart rate had vastly increased and her blood pressure was dangerously high.

Meanwhile in Megan's sleep the three emaciated dogs chased her again, trying to get to her. But Megan just couldn't run fast enough!

Megan, just wake up and it will all be gone, something deep inside her whispered. But she couldn't. The dogs growled, drooling as they snapped at her.

Just wake up. If I can open my eyes, it will all be gone! The dogs snapped again. Megan saw a group of people standing nearby but they wouldn't help her, they wouldn't respond to her cries. Finally she sprinted as fast as she could, but her sick heart was slowing her down. It wasn't enough...she was falling...she felt their breath on her neck...

She snapped her head against her pillow and her eyes popped open. She could feel her weak heart pounding with every bit of the energy it had.

"Megs, it's okay," her mom said urgently. "It's okay. I'm here."

As Megan's blood pressure dropped and her heart rate returned to normal, the nurse visibly sighed. "Whew! You had us worried there!" she told Megan, patting her arm.

When the nurse finally left the room, Megan swallowed and admitted to her mom, "It's the nightmares. They're horrible!"

She explained a little of what she was going through when her eyes were closed.

"Mom, why am I having all of these bad dreams?" Megan asked, trying not to sob. "Why do I keep seeing these bad creatures? I know you guys are always with me so why do I keep dreaming I'm alone and that no one will help me?"

Kathie thrust a tissue in Megan's hands and let her girl keep talking. "Is the devil trying to scare me and discourage me? Does he see everyone supporting me, so he's trying to destroy me through my dreams? I don't understand," she cried, giving way to the tears.

Kathie leaned in close to her daughter, wishing she could just make everything better. She wished she could be in the dreams with Megan to comfort her and help them disappear. But she couldn't.

However on the other hand, she knew Someone who could.

Kathie started praying. She prayed that God would send His angels to surround Megan's entire room. She prayed that Megan would feel comfortable. She asked God to give her precious daughter sweet sleep and pleasant dreams.

Then Kathie began quoting the Bible verses the Holy Spirit brought to her mind. Megan wouldn't remember all the verses later, but she'd remember how they comforted her heart.

Megan glanced at the clock. She was surprised to notice that they had been talking and praying for 45 minutes. She felt completely at peace as she reflected on one of the verses her mom had quoted, Psalm 4:8: "In peace I will lie down and sleep, for you alone, O LORD, will keep me safe."

The power of prayer and God's Word had transformed yet another situation. Never again did

Megan experience another nightmare or horrible vision during her hospital stay. The bad dreams were history.

Throughout the day, the family counted their blessings, but Megan's need for a heart always loomed before them. Megan had received another pint of blood; the doctors were still battling to properly balance the fluids in her body with the needs of the LVAD machine. The doctors also said that Monday would be the absolute deadline. If a heart was not available by then, Megan would have to have the internal LVAD surgery.

As Wayne and Kathie said goodnight prayers with Meg, they asked God to use Megan's suffering to bring people to know Jesus as their Savior. Although they focused on ministry and the abundance of blessings, they knew the facts were bleak.

Chapter 10

Faith if the Worst Happens

Saturday, April 10

* * * * *

It was a beautiful day in Room #12 of 56ICU. Megan's numbers were stable, the LVAD was working perfectly, and Megan was looking good. In fact, it was hard to believe she was being kept alive by a machine. Only her inability to get out of bed and her increased need for naps reminded the family that time was running out.

Sheryl knew that if today was anything like the previous Saturday, she would need to catch her time with her brother and Megan before visitors arrived at Barnes. So she arrived early and helped Megan primp for visitors, fed her some snacks, and enjoyed small talk with her chatty niece. When Megan began to look sleepy, Sheryl tucked the blanket snuggly under her chin.

It never fails, Sheryl thought, *time spent with Megan is always positive and uplifting.*

She marveled that this bedridden girl could be so pleasant even though she knew her days on earth were limited without a miracle. Sheryl read some of the emails that had come to Megan while Wayne updated the blog.

• 11:00 a.m. Meg is resting, and Sheryl and I are enjoying our view of Forest Park. It reminds us of "How Great our God Is." He has created all things, and yet He cares about Megan. *God, we plead with You today to bring healing and continued peace to Megan as she gives You praise in* all *things.* Megan's prayer is, "Lord, make me a sanctuary of praise." He is definitely answering that prayer. Doctors, nurses, everyone is in awe of Megan's spirit through this.

* * * * *

Megan had barely finished her lunch when the stream of visitors began. So many visitors arrived that Sharon manned the waiting room guest book while Sheryl and Shar rotated visitors in and out of Megan's room. Shar finally asked, "Megan, is this wearing you out too much?"

"No!" Megan exclaimed. "I want to see *everyone!*"

Finally, when just Kathie and Sharon were left in her room, Megan asked them to sing before she went to sleep. The three held hands and sang

Megan's favorite song about being the Lord's sanctuary.

Is that why she wanted to see everyone today? Sharon pondered. *I think so! She didn't want to miss an opportunity to be that living sanctuary!*

Megan still obviously believed in her motto: *Christ is enough—come what may!*

The future was so uncertain, but because Megan knew that Creator God was in charge, she could sleep in peace.

* * * * *

Sunday, April 11

Dr. Wang entered the room smiling. "Since Megan is doing so well, we have decided not to do surgery tomorrow. We'll let her remain on the external LVAD for one more week."

Staying on the LVAD this long was unheard of! Although Wayne and Kathie continued listening to the plans, their minds praised God for Megan's positive response to the LVAD. They believed God was in the process of answering prayers and performing Megan's miracle. They would continue to thank God for each day and for each mini miracle and blessing.

Dr. Wang was so proud of his model patient that he asked to take Megan's picture sitting in the shuttle chair. He wanted to share it at a conference on transplant patients the following week.

Megan was pleased to accommodate this nice doctor. The nurses slid Megan to the huge chair and helped her apply a little make-up and comb her hair. She looked good.

Dr. Wang had another request. A cardiologist friend from out of town wanted his daughter to interview Megan if she was up to it. The sixth-grader was doing a science project on the LVAD, and Dr. Wang suggested that seeing Megan and her machine would be helpful. Again, Megan was glad to accommodate.

Later that afternoon, the girl and her father arrived with their video camera. The sixth-grader asked Megan a few questions while her father videotaped Megan and the chair. Megan was sure that this girl would wow her teacher with her research, and through it, the Lord would be carrying her story to the girl's school in Wichita, Kansas, 500 miles away.

Throughout the day the medical personnel continued to be amazed at Megan's numbers. The day was filled with thankfulness that the mechanical heart would not be installed yet. The family had a few more days to pray for the miracle. Realistically they knew time was running out, but they chose to exercise faith instead of worry. They would hope for what was not seen, and believe for what they had not yet received.

* * * * *

Monday, April 12

Dr. Wang came early to give Megan and the family a report from the night's stats: everything looked great. He also mentioned that the Barnes Hospital Administrator would like to interview Megan.

"I'll be glad to meet him," she responded gracefully.

Although Megan's test reports looked great, the medical staff knew Megan's condition could worsen at any moment. If a donor heart did not come soon, the only option would be to give Megan the internal LVAD. In order to prepare Megan for this possibility, the staff member in charge of this specialized instrument came to show it to her.

Although Megan had heard about the internal LVAD and knew why she didn't want it, seeing it and realizing the nearness of the possibility was emotionally devastating. Megan couldn't imagine carrying a power pack everywhere. The IV pack she had carried during February and March could be hidden in a purse, and had been temporary. But having these huge batteries hooked to her for the rest of her life seemed awful.

Oh, God, please don't let it come to this! her broken heart cried.

The family soon decided that Megan had been through enough; she didn't need visitors that night.

In spite of her unsettled emotions, Megan's appetite was good. She also received some therapy time in the shuttle chair. Megan enjoyed the change in position so much that she was reluctant to go back to bed. Every time the nurse asked if she was ready, Megan responded, "Not yet." So she sat in the chair for two and a half hours.

Later that day Megan experienced severe chest pain. But thanks to the strong pain medication, Megan finally rested peacefully.

* * * * *

Wayne and Kathie spent a quiet evening floating between Megan's room and the waiting room. They thanked the visitors who came but explained Megan's need to rest. When the last visitor left, Kathie nestled in the recliner next to Megan's bed and fell asleep. Wayne was eager to get to bed at the Ritz.

As Sharon closed the day, she wondered if some of the prayer warriors were also weary and had let up on their praying, or if the family was simply feeling the weight of the physical and emotional strain that they had endured for twelve days. Whatever the reason, it had been a lonely, sad, difficult day for Megan and the family.

When Sharon arrived in Megan's room at 9:30 p.m. ready to assume night duty, Kathie was sleeping so soundly that Sharon decided not to disturb her.

It was almost midnight when Sharon checked on Kathie yet again. The nurse confirmed that neither Kathie nor Megan had moved a muscle. She encouraged Sharon to sleep in the consult room assuring her that she'd wake her to take over duty at Meg's side if Kathie as much as wiggled.

Sharon agreed. She returned to the waiting room to get her pillow and fleece blanket. She saw Debbie making her waiting-room bed, and asked, "How is your husband tonight?"

Sharon had exchanged many conversations with this young woman during recent days, and when Debbie wanted to know how Megan was, Sharon described the emotional, painful day that Megan had experienced.

"What will you do if God doesn't answer your prayers?" Debbie asked. "Your family is taking all of this so calmly; we are all amazed. You have such great faith in a God who answers your prayers, but how will you handle it if God lets Megan die?"

Sharon took a deep breath. "You would see us handle her death in the same way you have seen us handle the ups and downs of the last several days. Our faith is in God, not just in what we know He can do. Yes, God may choose to take Megan home to heaven. If so, you will see us cry; we are human! But, you will also see us continue to praise God knowing that He *always* loves us and will be faithful to us— no matter what."

Debbie admitted that she was struggling with her own faith. Sharon now knew that God had ordained her being awake at this moment in time. She sat down and spent two hours answering this spiritually hungry woman's questions about God and Christianity. The waiting room became a sanctuary when Sharon and Debbie prayed. As Sharon hugged this woman, she hoped she had successfully transferred her belief that God can be trusted, no matter what we face.

Chapter 11

Willing to Participate

Tuesday, April 13

* * * * *

Wayne wasn't sure how his birthday would
end, but it certainly didn't begin well. Dr. Wang
informed him that the insurance company
wouldn't cover the LVAD Megan needed. They
would cover the older, larger device but not the
newer, smaller device. Dr. Wang assured Wayne
that he would try to convince the insurance
company to honor his recommendation.

Wayne's morning at the hospital was otherwise
uneventful. He assisted Megan with drinks and
snacks, watched her sleep, talked with Sharon and
Sheryl, and read the many emails and Facebook
posts from friends wishing him, "Happy Birthday."

He also prayed and tried not to worry about Megan's medical need and his financial dilemma. There was no way he could pay for the device. He needed a miracle: insurance approval or a donor heart.

Now that Megan required so much pain medication, she slept a lot. In the quiet room, the hum of the pumping LVAD was a constant reminder that time was running out. As Wayne prayed by Meg's bed, he reflected on the biblical discipline of fasting, giving up food to pray. Due to his low blood sugar, he had fasted few times in his life. He wanted to ask readers to fast, but he wondered how he could ask others to do what he could not do. After much contemplation, hoping the Holy Spirit would lead some of his readers to pray and fast, he wrote:

• 5:00 p.m. The Doc tells us our time is running out and that Megan is still very critical. Next step is an internal LVAD, which comes with physical, emotional, and insurance issues. We need a healed or new heart by Monday. We are asking God's Family to follow God's lead as you pray on Megan's behalf for a *miracle*. "Keep on asking, and you will receive" Matthew 7:7.

* * * * *

Wayne's sisters made his waiting-room birthday party special with his favorite dessert: a multi-layered carrot cake. After thirteen days of emotional drain, however, he couldn't get into a party spirit. The basket of cards from the children at school only reminded him of what life used to be like. He laughed and wiped tears as he read the hand-written birthday wishes that were blended with prayers for Megan.

The day held one bright spot, though. After reading the blog, a newcomer to Wayne's church felt that God wanted him to plan a prayer vigil for Friday night from 10:00 to 11:00 to be held at the North County Christian School parking lot.

Wayne left for the hotel, Kathie made her bed in the consultation room, and Sharon took the night shift by Megan's bed. Megan had repeatedly mentioned how it gave her peace just knowing that she was never alone, even while she was sleeping.

I am being God with skin on! Sharon thought.

Before trying to sleep, Kathie needed to connect with her praying friends on Facebook: "10:20 p.m. I tried to pray this afternoon; just couldn't find any words, so I got my Bible to pray the Word. This is what He gave me: 'Be still in the presence of the LORD, and wait patiently for Him to act' (Psalm 37:7), and 'He has given me a new song to sing, a hymn of praise to our God. Many will see what He has done and be amazed. They will put their trust in the LORD' (Psalm 40:3)."

As Kathie pondered these verses, she was reminded that God was currently in the process of performing His miracle; she only had to be patient. And, ultimately this miracle—this whole journey—was not just about Megan; it was about those God wanted to bring to Himself.

* * * * *

Wednesday, April 14

Megan woke early when the sun peeped through the horizontal window blinds. She suddenly realized she'd slept most of the day before and still slept throughout the night.

I wonder if God is letting me get rested so I'm ready to receive my new heart today!

She was in a good mood and didn't seem to mind the many tests the staff ordered.

The family wasn't as positive as Megan. God hadn't answered their prayers in the way they wanted the day before—no miracle heart became available and no miracle call from the insurance company. They were weary, and it was becoming more difficult to believe that all would end well. Their hearts hurt for precious Megan who was becoming thinner every day.

Wayne periodically checked the blog and his Facebook account and read Megan's email cards. He was encouraged by how many friends were fasting today. There was no way he could respond to each message of love and support. The blog entry would have to do:

• 10:20 a.m. While Megan is sleeping this morning, hundreds of family and friends are fasting and praying for her healing. We are again in awe of the Family of God and the way they are lifting Megan and the family in prayer. I don't even know how to pray sometimes, but I do know that Megan is God's child, too, and as her Father, He will do what is best for her. *I'm trusting You, God, to take care of our girl.*

* * * * *

A public relations staff member from Barnes entered Megan's room. He explained, "Kay Quinn, the anchor from Channel 5, wants to interview Megan."

Megan clarified, "You mean she wants to interview my dad?"

"No, she wants to interview you."

Megan thought for a moment and said, "Sure. How long do I have to get ready?"

"You'll probably have about two hours."

Wayne was surprised that Megan agreed to the interview since she was having more difficulty breathing, but Megan sincerely wanted the watching world to know the source of her strength: Jesus Christ.

However, only five minutes later, Kay Quinn appeared in Megan's room.

She must have been in the lobby, Wayne thought, asking Kay if she could wait a few minutes while they helped Megan finish getting ready. The nurse hurriedly brushed Megan's hair into a ponytail and Sheryl applied some blush and mascara. In spite of her struggle to breathe, Megan gave an awesome fourteen-minute interview. Wayne was amazed at how God was advertising Megan's story.

Although Megan breathed heavily all day, she tried to eat. She also watched a lot of TV since her television was set on Channel 5 in anticipation of the news broadcasts.

By now, the waiting room family had enlarged. When the five o'clock news came on, both televisions were set to Channel 5 and all the family and new friends watched the news, clapping and shouting, "Yeah, Megan," when the interview ended.

Megan's family was proud of their girl and prayed with all their hearts that God would use the interview to bring others to faith and make people aware of the need for donors.

* * * * *

Although Shar's husband, Charlie, had returned home to California, he and Shar had kept in constant contact through text messages and calls.

When Shar answered her cell phone that night, Charlie explained, "Shar, when I got dressed this morning, I put on a shirt you bought for me years ago that I'd never worn.

"When I got home tonight I emptied all of my pockets and found a small, stuffed purple heart." That did not surprise him. Shar was always sticking love notes in his socks, pockets, and among his other clothing.

But the more he looked at the heart, the more he believed it had significance for today. It was a symbol to him of Megan's need for a heart. He continued, "As I held the heart and prayed for Megan, I realized there was also a note in that pocket."

The note said, "There comes a point when we have to decide if we're willing to participate in a miracle–to possess the promise."

Shar was as astounded as Charlie by the timing of the note and its relevant message. Shar had begun her habit of hiding notes when she was a teenager. She always prayed that God would help the family member find the note exactly when it was needed. But this was unbelievable. This shirt had been in Charlie's closet for *four* years, but all the time it held relevant instruction for this very day.

Before Charlie went to sleep that night, he told his sister, Yolanda, about the extraordinary note. This brother and sister wanted a miracle and wanted to possess the promise of a heart for Megan, but they weren't sure what *they* could do to participate in the miracle.

* * * * *

Thursday, April 15

The next morning, still feeling burdened to participate in Megan's miracle, Yolanda visited a minister at her church. She asked, "What can I do to show God my willingness to participate in this miracle that Megan Moss needs?"

After thinking, the minister shared about several biblical accounts where people fasted to demonstrate their commitment of faith.

Yes! That's what I need to do! Yolanda decided.

When she shared her plan to fast with Charlie, he took it to the next level—the cyberspace level. He decided that since the gentleman in St. Louis had scheduled a prayer vigil for Friday night, it would be appropriate to call for a fast on Saturday.

Charlie opened his Facebook account and posted an Open Invitation to an Event. "What? A Day of Prayer and Fasting. When? Saturday, April 17th from 7:30 a.m. to 7:30 p.m. Where? All Over the World." With one click, the message literally went all over the world.

Charlie was thankful that he had such a long list of Facebook friends—including many he didn't even know. So within hours, friends of friends of friends were posting the event and sending it to their friends, families, churches, universities, and missionaries all over the world. People who didn't even know Megan decided to participate in a miracle by fasting on Saturday, April 17th.

When Shar told Megan about the note and the Day of Prayer and Fasting that God was organizing, Megan said, "Aunt Shar, we need that quote about participating in a miracle on my wall. Would you please put it on a card and hang it?"

Wayne believed that God was already honoring all of the prayer and fasting that had occurred. He needed to thank the blog followers:

• 11:30 a.m. Megan is sleeping well between interruptions. Good news: the insurance approved the smaller LVAD. We are thankful but still praying for God to heal her heart or provide a donor before Monday morning. We are believing, praying, and *expecting a miracle!*

* * * * *

Throughout the day, Megan found breathing more and more difficult. The nurse gave her a large, tighter oxygen mask that seemed to help, but Wayne and Kathie saw this as one step closer to the end of the LVAD days. Their only comfort came from knowing that the next two days would be covered with prayer: the Friday Night Prayer Vigil and now the Saturday Day of Prayer and Fasting.

* * * * *

116

While Kathie and Wayne struggled watching their daughter try to breathe, Sharon was unexpectedly thrust into her own emotional dilemma.

She remained in the waiting room on baby-watching duty that evening while Shar visited with Megan and her parents. While Sharon watched Grayeson, a visitor decided to unburden her heart by telling Sharon about a dream she had. Unfortunately, the woman had dreamed about Sharon's 35-year-old daughter, Karen.

This woman shared that she had dreamed Karen was on the way to St. Louis with her two boys to see Megan—only to have a terrible accident. Since Karen had signed her license to be an organ donor, Karen's heart had been flown to Barnes and given to Megan.

"I had an awful spiritual battle when I woke up," the woman said. "I couldn't imagine you having to give up one family member to save the life of another."

With more tears she directed a question to Sharon, "God couldn't possibly want that, could He?"

Sharon had hidden her shock and dismay as she'd continued to play with Grayeson during the story. Now Sharon swallowed hard and stoically answered, "He may want us to just be willing."

Grayeson's restlessness ended the conversation, but Sharon's internal discussion was far from over. Karen was a healthy, female family member with the same blood type as Megan, and she was only twelve years older than her cousin. Karen's heart would probably be a perfect match.

Karen had been trying to get away from her home 850 miles away to come to the hospital, but she had not yet been able to leave. As Sharon thought about her daughter traveling that far, in light of the woman's dream, she felt like she'd been punched in the chest and her insides heaved with pain while she struggled to outwardly maintain composure.

Sharon's cell phone rang. Ironically, it was Karen on the line.

Sharon couldn't get a clear phone line in the waiting room, so she passed Grayeson to a friend and gratefully dashed to the part of the hospital that offered the best cell reception.

"Hi, Karen."

"Mom, I don't know if I'm supposed to make this trip or not. I've had to postpone it so many times. The boys and I are feeling fine, but the mechanic called today and they won't be able to get the part until tomorrow; it will be late tomorrow evening before we can pick up the van. If I come, it won't be until Saturday morning."

While Karen was talking, Sharon's mind was reviewing the dream and silently asking God to help her know what to say—and most importantly, what not to say to Karen. Sharon clearly felt that God did not want her to live in fear of a dream or transfer that fear to Karen. So, she kept the awful dream to herself and chose to let *God* stall or prevent Karen's trip. She simply told Karen, "I'll be praying that God will make it very clear to you about if and when you should come."

Sharon was on autopilot, keeping the woman's dream a secret and camouflaging her heavy heart until she made her bed in the consultation room that night.

In the privacy of the dark room, Sharon's mind rehearsed the account of the dreadful dream. Her spirit was heavy as she contemplated what God might require of her as she chose to participate in Megan's miracle.

Sharon decided first of all not to tell anyone about the dream; she would not speak her fear. She then prayed and wrestled with her willingness to participate in Megan's miracle. If participation meant more prayer, she could do that. If it meant fasting, she could even do without food for a few days.

But to give her daughter's heart?

She knew she couldn't say "yes" to this possible participation lightly.

Sharon humanly explained away the possibility of this dream coming true by thinking, *An 850-mile trip is a long trip with two children, but Karen is a good driver and has made several long trips before.*

But Sharon was checked in her spirit. She knew God did not want her to spend time denying the possibility of an accident, and neither did He want her to beg Him to prevent the accident the lady saw in her dream. Instead, as she prayed, Sharon felt God was using the dream to clarify Sharon's level of trust and surrender to His will.

After Sharon gave God all the reasons why using Karen's heart would not be a good choice for Him to make, she began her surrender as she cried out to God, "I trust You...come what may. I will not tell You how, and I will not withhold *anything* from You. God, You can have whatever You need from me in order to transfer my faith to the next generation. I can't imagine the pain that Tony, Garrett and Logan would experience, but God I trust You. And, only You, God, know how much I love Karen; she is not only my daughter, she's my very best friend. But nevertheless, Your will be done!"

For months Sharon had been praying for the donor family and wanted God to help them and comfort them. On this night, however, as she struggled with surrender, she realized that she could not ask another mother to do what she was unwilling to do.

As Sharon sobbed, her surrender became complete. She was not saying that she loved Megan more than Karen. She didn't even feel God had trapped her into surrendering out of fear or guilt. She realized that her faith had taught her to fully trust the One who loved her, and that peace comes only through trust and unconditional surrender.

Sharon finally went to sleep knowing that her surrender was complete. In her own spiritual and emotional heart, she realized that for her, as for Megan, Christ was enough—come what may!

Chapter 12

Countdown Clock Nears Midnight

Friday, April 16

* * * * *

Throughout the night Megan's breathing became even more labored. She grew weaker, and the medical staff confirmed that the vital numbers weren't as good. Even though the incredible machine was doing its part, Megan's heart was giving its last quivering attempts at beating.

Kathie spent more time at Meg's bedside that night; she was tired and the prospects of the day did not look hopeful. When she passed the baton of duty to Wayne and Sharon that morning, the two adjusted Megan's oxygen mask, fluffed her pillow, and gently massaged her swollen legs.

Mandi arrived earlier than usual and helped care for Megan as physicians and technicians entered and exited the room. Mandi noticed that everyone talked more quietly than normal; and she didn't think it was just because Megan was sleeping. Mandi held Meg's hand and prayed that God would spare the life of her sister, her best friend.

Shortly after Kathie returned from the hotel, Megan's doctor verified Mandi's instincts. Because Megan's heart was not strong enough to work even with the LVAD, her body systems were shutting down. Fluid was building rapidly around her heart and lungs. They needed to insert a tube in Megan's chest hoping the fluids would drain and ease her breathing. Because Megan needed to be weaned from the blood thinners for four hours, the bedside procedure was set for late afternoon.

Dr. Wang explained the risks of this procedure to Megan's family: excessive bleeding and cessation of breathing.

When the doctor left the room, the family stood silently by Meg. They had promised not to be negative in Megan's room, but this situation did not look good.

Wayne turned again to the concerned people who checked the blog each day. He was assured that friends would again carry Megan's needs to God in prayer:

• 10:00 a.m. Meg is struggling to breathe this morning. Going to have to do a surgical procedure this afternoon to relieve fluid around her lungs and heart. Also white blood count is rising which could mean infection. *God, it is so hard to watch Meg fighting for her life. Please, God, we need a miracle, a donor heart, soon!*

I need a place to cry and pray! Sharon thought. She told Wayne and Kathie she was going to the prayer chapel. They followed her, leaving Mandi with Megan.

Without speaking, they spaced themselves throughout the chapel to have a semblance of privacy. Although they could not hear each other's prayers as they bent over the blue padded chairs, they did hear the weeping.

"Oh, God, give Wayne and Kathie strength; give them peace; comfort their hurting hearts," Sharon cried.

Megan could really die today, she thought. *But how would her death fit into God's plan?*

"God, we didn't tell the world. You did!" She reminded God, "What will the Channel 4 and Channel 5 viewers and blog readers think? There are so many skeptics. God, they're watching to see if You really are a God of miracles.

"For Meg, and for my brother and his family, but God, especially for the unsaved who need to know You, please perform Your miracle so people will come to know You as we do!"

The three prayed until their words and weeping were spent. For several more minutes they rested in the quietness of the chapel before returning to 56ICU.

* * * * *

Wayne, Kathie, and the family received strength through this difficult day by knowing God was calling people from all over the world to pray for

123

their Meg. Many friends of all faiths planned to meet that night in the North County Christian School parking lot for public prayer and praise.

"Praise?" the skeptics had said. "At a time like this? In these circumstances?"

It was a fact that Megan's physical heart would not last much longer; it was dying. Nevertheless, the miracle-working God of the universe was still alive and well. The Christians who were following the blog and who were gathering believed with all their hearts that they served a faithful God who could heal Megan's diseased heart or provide a donor heart in time.

So in this hour of emotional darkness, they would continue to praise God for His faithfulness, no matter the outcome of Megan's physical body. They would pray in faith believing, but they would not demean God with demands. When you fully trust the One in charge, you ask and ask boldly, but you leave the results with the One you trust.

* * * * *

Wayne's sisters were helping with the prayer vigil, so they turned the table in the waiting room kitchenette into office space. Sharon brought her journal and Bible, and the three sisters began recalling the events, miracles, and blessings that had brought them to this place: the 16th day of the faith journey that had begun on April 1st when Megan was admitted for her third stay at Barnes.

Occasionally Wayne and Kathie added to the growing list of blessings: a hot meal provided by friends, gift cards to the hospital cafeteria, parking passes for the garage, emails, cards, blog comments, phone calls, scriptures, songs, and visits.

Hindsight proved that the timing of everything was the incredible providence of God: the timing of decisions, procedures, and surgeries; the timing of the arrival of friends and family; the scriptures that came via text messaging, email, and in the guest book; the songs that were sung in Megan's room. God used all of these timely blessings to lift their spirits.

"How could we possibly give God all the praise that He deserves?" they exclaimed.

Even though they didn't understand why Megan had to suffer and had no idea whether or not God would spare her life, the family around that table praised God through their tears.

As his sisters planned for the vigil, Wayne sat with Meg, feeding her ice chips and calming her when the oxygen mask became uncomfortable. He also prayed and read from Joshua 6 how the impenetrable walls of Jericho tumbled when Joshua and the Israelites obeyed God's command to march around the city.

Joshua and the Israelites had to truly believe that God would be faithful to His word for they continued to daily obey God's instructions even though they didn't see evidence that the miracle would happen. On the seventh day and the seventh trip around the walls, they obeyed God's command to shout and the walls came down.

Wayne realized anew that the Israelites put their faith in God's plan, not in their own abilities. He had an idea: he would claim the territory around Megan's bed. His walk of faith around

Meg's ICU bed would not be a magical, ceremonial walk. His walk of obedience would simply demonstrate his trust in the Almighty God who had a plan for his daughter.

*　*　*　*　*

As the day progressed, Megan's breathing became more labored. With each breath, Megan's chest lifted dramatically and her head jerked backward into her pillow. Wayne and Kathie cried as they watched their daughter gasping for each breath.

Kathie repeatedly played the song "Draw Me Near" on her computer as she caressed Meg's hand and adjusted the cloth that shielded Meg's eyes from the light. Wayne, Kathie, and Mandi sensed that God had chosen to reside in this very room because He dwelled within their hearts. He was very near.

Late in the afternoon, Wayne received a call from Channel 5 TV. "We read on your blog that there will be a prayer vigil for Megan tonight. We would like to cover it live on the 10:00 news."

"That will be fine," he said. "Since Megan is so bad, though, Kathie and I won't be there. But my sisters will be there early to show you where to set up."

Wayne was amazed at yet more media coverage. The family prayed throughout the rest of the day that God would receive glory throughout the nations as He advertised Himself once again. God was truly putting His reputation on the line as Megan's story and need of a miracle were broadcast via television, and thereby the internet, around the world.

* * * * *

It was nearing 5:30 p.m.

The medical team was almost ready for the in-room surgical procedure that would again puncture Megan's already perforated body. One doctor expressed his hope that they would be able to keep Megan breathing while under the anesthetic so she wouldn't suffer the trauma of a respirator.

Family members wiped spontaneous tears. Megan was aware of their anxiety and had her own concerns. She could sense that her strength was weakening. She wasn't one to admit her fear, but she silently contemplated the grim fact that her end could be very near, and she knew that this procedure increased that risk.

Again Megan led her family in this faith journey. With confidence that God was the One in charge of her miracle story, she whispered from beneath the oxygen mask. "Mom, all my life...you've taught me...to pray specifically...for what I really...needed."

"Yes, Megan. I have."

"Then Mom...will you ask...the family...and the...Facebook friends...to pray...that I will feel Jesus...holding me...during the procedure?"

"Yes, I will ask them to pray specifically." Kathie took a deep breath. She did believe God would answer this heartfelt request. She opened her laptop and invited friends and family to participate in yet another opportunity for God to show His compassion.

Kathie's Facebook post read: "5:41 p.m. *Please pray* right now. Getting ready to begin procedure of placing a chest tube. Meg has asked that we pray that Jesus will hold her in His arms and keep her at peace."

Since only two could stay, Kathie and Mandi remained. Wayne kissed his precious girl and walked mournfully from her room.

What if that's my last good-bye to Megan?

With uncontrollable sobs, Wayne stumbled to the waiting room.

Through his tears Wayne caught a glimpse of God's great love when he spotted the family's friend Val sitting quietly. Wayne knew God had prompted her to come to the hospital for this very moment. This was the same Val who was sent by God at the very moment when he and Kathie had received the devastating news on Saturday, April 3, that the LVAD surgery was the only hope of saving Megan's life; Val, the mom whose teenage daughter survived a year of being in and out of St. Louis Children's Hospital as she fought leukemia and won. Val believed in miracles and knew how to comfort Wayne as Jesus would. Again, God was faithful in Wayne's time of need.

* * * * *

The procedure went well, and Megan could breathe without a respirator. Somewhere in between the ice chips and subdued conversation, Megan suddenly lifted her head and shoulders.

"Mom, did you ask them...to pray...like I said?" She excitedly asked.

Mom responded, "Yes, Meg, we did. We asked all of the Facebook friends to pray that you would feel Jesus holding you." Still watching the astonished look on Meg's face, she asked, "So, Meg, did you feel Jesus?"

"I did!" Meg exclaimed with a surprisingly strong voice.

"What was it like?" Mom asked.

With a calm smile and arms folded across her chest, Meg whispered, "Jesus held me...and squeezed me...just like this."

With tears of praise, Kathie told her Facebook friends: "Thanks for praying. Procedure went well...Jesus held Meg! Anticipating a miracle tonight."

Meg playing highschool
basketball before myocarditis.

Meg and Jason jet skiing during
summer vaction in 2004.

Kissing "Tyler" the dolph
in Orlando, FL in 2008.

Thanksgiving Day 2009...
The Moss Family:
Megan, Kathie, Wayne,
Kyle, Mandi, Kinsley,
Dani & Jason.

...st weeks after the
...efibrillator surgery,
...legan poses for a
...hristmas photo
...nat later becomes
...ie icon for the
...legan's Heart
...tory blog.

Kathie watches as
Mark Schnyder of
Channel 4, KMOV-
TV interviews
Wayne in the Barnes
Hospital Cafeteria
on Easter Sunday,
the day after the
LVAD surgery.

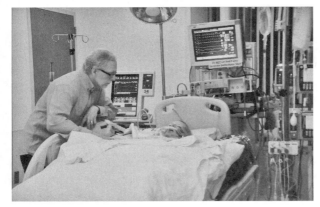

Wayne looking down on Megan following the LVAD surgery.

As an escape from the bed, Megan sits in the shuttle chair.

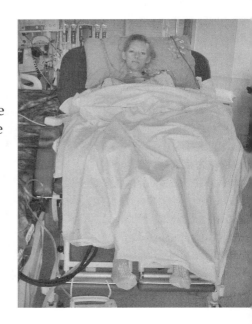

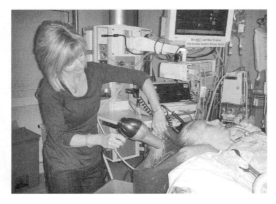

Megan is feeling much better after the nurse and Kathie wash and dry her hair.

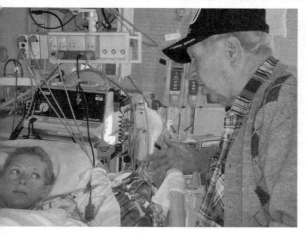

Megan listens intently as Grandpa Moss shares his wisdom and encouragement.

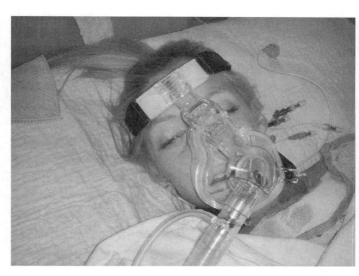

Megan struggles to breathe on the no-hope, dilemma-filled Saturday (April 17) when the medical staff determined that they had done all they could do.

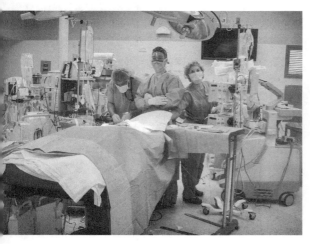

The operating room staff makes last-minute preparations for Megan's heart transplant.

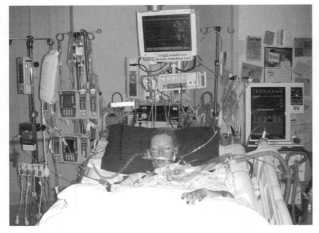

While Megan is in a chemically induced sleep following the transplant, the family contemplates the news of the possible stroke during surgery.

Following the transplant, Megan's new heart beats like her own, but she is still surrounded by tubes and machines.

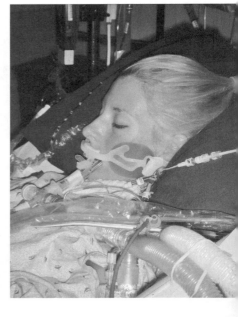

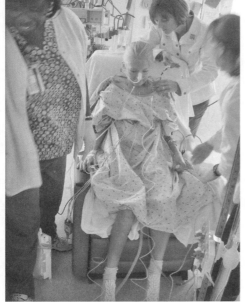

Megan is overwhelmed by how difficult it is to stand for the first time.

The Heartfelt Celebration as seen from Megan's 5th-floor ICU room.

The feeding tube delivers nutrition to Meg, and Mandi enjoys hanging out with her sister.

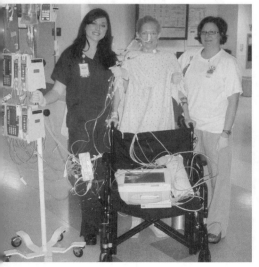

Megan knows she is on the road to recovery when she takes her first lap around the ICU unit.

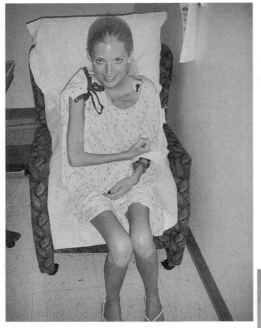

As Megan prepares to dress for her trip home, she realizes how thin she has become. Now that she has a new heart, she has to work on gaining weight and muscle mass.

Megan has just finished her "almost-ready-to-go-home" interview with Channel 5, and Dr. Wang, her transplant surgeon, celebrates with her.

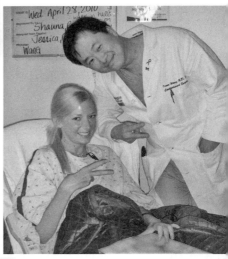

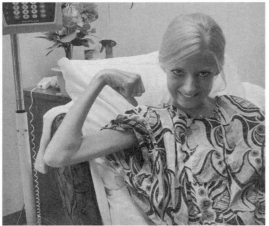

While in the step-down unit in preparation for home-care, Megan shows off her muscle and her brightly-colored gown, a gift from Auntie Shar.

In June 2010, Megan is excited to be wearing heels for the first time since being diagnosed.

Megan speaks at the St. Louis Go Red for Women luncheon in February 2011.

Feeling better than ever, Megan marries her best friend, Nathan Johnson, in October 2011.

Chapter 13

Outpourings of Prayer

Friday, April 16

* * * * *

The Channel 5 truck parked on the North
County Christian School parking lot could be seen
from I-270. Cars, vans, trucks, and SUVs streamed
in. The Moss family recognized many people, but
some strangers had seen the event posted on the
blog and showed up to investigate or participate.

One young woman asked a family member,
"Why a prayer vigil tonight? The girl is still alive
isn't she?"

The family member responded, "Yes, Megan is
still alive. Our purpose for this vigil is to not only
ask God for a miracle, but we want to praise Him
for what He has already done and what we believe
He can still do."

By the time the watches and smart phones
displayed 10:00 p.m., more than a hundred men,

women, and children had gathered holding candles that lit the darkness.

"We've gathered tonight to pray for Megan Moss who desperately needs a new heart," the leader, Jim, announced. "Her aunts, Sheryl and Shar, will read scriptures and will lead us in songs and prayer. We are here to ask God for a miracle, but we are also here to praise Him for His faithfulness."

After she thanked people for coming, Sheryl said, "During the last several months, my family has received comfort from God's Word. We don't know what God wants to do regarding Megan's need for a new heart, but we do know that His Word tells us to ask in faith believing."

Sheryl told how God had given Kathie a promise from Ezekiel 36:23 (NIV) just a few days after Megan's congestive heart failure diagnosis in November. The scripture said, "Then the nations will know that I am the LORD, declares the Sovereign LORD, when I show myself holy through *you* before their eyes."

Sheryl exclaimed to the group, "This scripture is being fulfilled! Through technology, God is taking Megan's need for a heart and the story of her faith to the nations. Megan is living her motto: Through her suffering she is *demonstrating that Christ is enough—come what may!*"

She read scriptures that God had used to comfort and assure the family. Then Sheryl explained how they would pray, "I will describe a need and we will pray for that request. You may pray silently, pray aloud, or pray in groups; just pray however God leads you.

"First we will ask God to heal Megan's diseased heart and make it like new...*if* that will bring Him the most glory."

She led the group in specific prayer that Megan's swelling would go away, that her left ventricle would heal, that the right ventricle would be strengthened. The group prayed that Megan would be protected from infection, that her organs would create a perfect balance of fluids, and that her body would have the proper blood flow.

Some bowed their heads, others looked toward the sky. Some whispered their prayers, others cried out to the Great Physician.

The group broke from prayer to sing some of Megan's favorite faith-filled songs. Then they returned to prayer for the medical staff, that God would work in such a way that the staff would know it was a miracle.

After the next song, Sheryl told the group about one of her father's sayings: "Remember, the brink of a disaster and the brink of a miracle are at the same spot."

She added, "To most, Meg's worsening condition appears to be a disaster. But we believe Meg's condition is even more of an opportunity for God to show Himself mighty and show us, and an unbelieving world, a miracle."

Sheryl reminded everyone that the family wanted God's will, no matter what. Although the healing of Megan's heart would be easier on her body, they realized that God might heal her through a transplant.

"If God chooses to give Megan a donor heart, then we need to pray for the donor family," she said. "Let's pray that the donor family who has the perfect-match heart to give will have peace about their decision. Pray that God will meet their every need during this time of personal grief."

Sheryl read Kathie's promise for the day from Psalm 109:26-27: "Help me, O LORD my God! Save me because of your unfailing love. Let them see that this is your doing, that you yourself have done it, LORD."

And then Psalm 40:3: "He has given me a new song to sing, a hymn of praise to our God. Many will see what he has done and be amazed. They will put their trust in the LORD."

As the vigil ended, Shar told the story of Charlie finding the four-year-old note in his shirt. She continued, "I don't know what God might want you to do to participate in this miracle, but just obey Him. You might want to join the hundreds of others around the world who will fast and pray tomorrow from 7:30 a.m. to 7:30 p.m. If you cannot fast, for whatever reason, please continue to pray with us."

As Sheryl led the group in a closing prayer, a father and six-year-old son knelt together on the cold asphalt. Families cried out in prayer together. Couples embraced and wept. And an elderly woman raised her hands toward heaven as tears ran down her wrinkled cheeks.

Finally, people blew out their candles and the darkness returned, but they were not consumed by it. The new commitment to participate in Megan's miracle had given them renewed hope that the miracle was on the way.

* * * * *

Megan had her TV on Channel 5 all evening, eager to see the 10:00 p.m. news. The coverage of the prayer vigil was brief but was another opportunity to get the word out: "Help us pray! Megan needs a heart!"

Soon after watching the news coverage, Megan needed another chest x-ray. Since she was breathing better, everyone hoped the x-ray would show that the tube had decreased the fluid around the heart.

Knowing the prayer vigil was still in progress, Wayne, Kathie, and Sharon left the room during the x-ray procedure and found an empty room where they could have their own vigil.

When they returned to Megan's room, the three stood by her bed and sang worship songs and witnessed another mini-miracle. Between gasps of breath, Meg tried to sing with them. She still chose to praise the God she loved in spite of her circumstances.

Wayne and Sharon didn't want to leave Meg's bedside that night. The ticking clock seemed to keep getting louder even though they tried to ignore it. But God gave Kathie peace. She reminded Wayne and Sharon, "I will stay with Meg, but we *all* need to trust the angels to care for her tonight so we can sleep."

Kathie settled into the recliner in Megan's room; Wayne finally fell asleep in the hotel bed. Sharon found her familiar place on the love-seat in the consult room. She thought, *This day definitely produced some significant Ebenezer stones!* She prayed, "Jesus, help Wayne, Kathie, Meg and me to sleep exceptionally well; and, wake us prepared to participate in the possession of the miracle. Do Your radical, surgical healing of Meg's heart or provide a *perfect heart* in Jesus' name. I rest in *You!* What an incredibly uplifting but difficult day!"

The countdown clock set in motion almost two weeks earlier by the LVAD surgery was now nearing midnight. As the family sought sleep they were well aware of the physical reality: time was up and only a miracle would do.

Chapter 14

We Waited Too Long

Saturday, April 17

* * * * *

Sharon woke suddenly at 6:20 a.m. feeling impressed to get up. After inserting her contacts she retrieved her vibrating phone. The 6:26 a.m. text message from Kathie read, "Meg having difficulty breathing."

Sharon hurried to Megan's room. Kathie explained, "Meg had a restless night. Early this morning her breathing became more labored. At about 6:20 she began struggling to breathe again."

As Sharon stood by her gasping niece, she felt inadequate to give Kathie comfort. As she prayed silently, though, she became consumed with the wonder of God's adequacy. He loved Meg and her family enough to have Charlie and Yolanda plan the Day of Prayer and Fasting for *this* very day. *Thank you, God! Those prayers will be our comfort and strength today!*

As Sharon thought about the 7:30 a.m. to 7:30 p.m. fast, she looked at the clock; it was 6:40 a.m. in St. Louis, but it was 7:40 a.m. on the East Coast. Ten minutes earlier East Coast friends, family, and even many strangers had begun praying. She was convinced the timing was not circumstantial.

Kathie left Sharon with Megan while she called Wayne and asked Facebook friends to pray.

During the morning rounds, the doctors changed medications and ordered more blood tests and x-rays. They adjusted the flow of the LVAD and increased Megan's Lasix intake to help her eliminate fluids. Within a short while, Meg's numbers improved a bit.

Wayne opened his laptop to call for worldwide prayer.

Shortly before 10:00 a.m., Dr. Wang arrived to deliver the results of the many tests. The chest x-ray showed pneumonia, and Megan's temperature had climbed to 102 degrees. The LVAD was chattering, an indication that Megan's heart was so far gone that her body lacked adequate blood flow to support the LVAD process. All body systems were beginning to fail.

When Dr. Wang left the room, Wayne followed him, but Kathie stayed, looking at her daughter's almost lifeless body. Then she did what some moms would consider unthinkable: she left for her regular morning clean-up time at the Ritz. Kathie reasoned that her presence did not help sleeping Meg, and her pounding heart told her that she *had* to find a place to pray—a place where she could cry out to God...*loudly*. So, she waved as she walked by Dr. Wang and Wayne and headed to the hotel.

Wayne continued his conversation with Dr. Wang. "I need more information," he said. "Because Megan's body systems are failing, does this mean if a heart came today, she would not be able to receive it?"

Dr. Wang responded, "That is correct. I'm so sorry, but we waited too long."

He explained that not only was Megan too sick to receive a transplant, he wasn't sure she was strong enough to receive a mechanical heart. The best they could hope for was to get the infection under control so she would *possibly* be strong enough to receive the internal LVAD on Monday. Dr. Wang indicated that they could do nothing else.

"You may not be able to do anything else medically, but we can still pray," Wayne said. "And we will!"

"That's all you can do," Dr. Wang agreed.

The medical staff now realized that prayer and a miracle were Megan's only hope.

Besides infection, the doctors faced other dilemmas. To increase the LVAD effectiveness, Megan desperately needed more blood. Although a unit of blood might improve the LVAD output, it would possibly cause fluid to build more rapidly around her heart and lungs. The extra fluid then would require an increase in Lasix which could seriously compromise her failing kidneys.

To further complicate matters, if her pneumonia-filled lungs couldn't breathe due to excessive fluid build-up, a full respirator would have to be inserted which would add to Megan's discomfort and increase the stress on her traumatized body.

After carefully weighing all the risks, however, the team of doctors chose to give Megan the unit of blood.

Kathie didn't know the no-hope, dilemma-filled details yet, and Wayne didn't want to give them to her through a text or call; but he did want the blog followers to intensify their praying.

How should I word the blog entry? he pondered. Then a song came to mind. That's what he would do. He would turn the readers' hearts to worship and ask them to claim the healing that he believed was still possible even though all the resources of medical science were nearly exhausted. He downloaded the link to include in the blog and wrote:

• 10:06 a.m. Family of God, this is my prayer for my baby today. Turn your volume up and cry out in worship to Him, and claim healing for Megan. "I Am the God that Healeth Thee" –Don Moen.

As soon as Wayne finished the entry, he uploaded the song, and it became the background music for Sharon's and his Jericho-wall marching and praying the rest of the morning. They tried to keep praying positively, but the spirits of darkness seemed to hover in the room. In all the previous days of uncertainty, the sense of death and darkness had never been this near. While their hearts wanted to believe for a miracle, they wondered if Megan was losing her battle for life.

At one point, Megan opened her eyes and whispered, "Is Mandi coming? Is Jason coming?" A few moments later, she struggled to speak again. "Are Grandma and Grandpa coming?"

Megan's dad assured her that they would all be there.

Sharon held Megan's frail hand, and she returned to sleep. Wayne left to look for Sheryl. When he found her in the waiting room he said, "Meg is failing fast. Please call Shar and tell her to bring Mom and Dad but not to let them know how badly Meg is doing. Call the others, too."

* * * * *

Megan slept, oblivious to her surroundings and the death angel that seemed to hover over the room. She now weighed just over 80 pounds and appeared to be a very young, malnourished teen. Although Meg's breathing was slightly improved, she slept with her eyes partially open. With every passing minute, she looked more like death.

Between answering and sending text messages, Wayne joined Sharon as she circled Meg's bed and prayed. And then, Sharon's daughter, Karen, called. "We left Virginia early this morning."

The dreadful dream the woman had told her about rushed into Sharon's consciousness. *Would the dream come true? Would Karen have an accident on her way to St. Louis? Would her heart be given to Megan today?"*

Karen continued, "I plan to stay in Indiana tonight. I'll get to St. Louis tomorrow evening."

Sharon recalled her agonizing prayer of surrender. Since her surrender to God's will *no matter what* had been made, she told her daughter, "Have a safe trip. Be sure to stop before you get to your brother's if you're getting too tired."

Sharon would have to trust Karen...and Megan...and their hearts into God's faithful hands.

Wayne walked to the window that overlooked Forest Park. In the distance he could see the Ritz. He thought of the employees there who loved Megan. Many of these were following the blog, waiting to see if Megan's God really answered prayers.

Wayne focused on the Clayton skyline and The Ritz-Carlton Hotel as he prayed. *God, my surrender is complete; Megan is Yours. But, I beg You to spare her for the sake of Your reputation.*

He wept for the unbelievers at the Ritz, the watching medical staff, the relatives who still needed Jesus, and the waiting room full of new friends who wondered if God would really answer the prayers of this family.

Oh, God, he prayed in desperation, *so many are watching to see if You can perform a miracle. Don't let people lose faith in You because of this. If You choose to take Megan today, show us what we can do to convince these people that You are real.*

Wayne left the window and stood by the wall that displayed Megan's encouragement cards. He touched each scripture card and turned each into a prayer. He believed in the power of praying God's Word and that God was listening and would answer.

* * * * *

Within the privacy of the hotel room, Kathie chose the white bathroom as her place of sanctuary, hoping that running water would camouflage her loud crying.

141

"God, unless You perform a miracle, my Megs is dying," she cried. "There's no hope except in Jesus! Oh, Jesus, help us."

She wept and groaned, but all she could say was, "Oh, Jesus. Oh, Jesus."

Finally she composed herself enough to address God.

"Father," she wept, "I don't even know how to present my request to You this morning. Over the last few months, I've prayed it all. You know I want You to spare Meg's life, but You also know I fully trust You. I can't even find words to say to You. Oh, God, please help me know how to pray."

In a kind, gentle voice in her mind she heard God whisper, *Child, just praise Me. Just praise Me.*

Kathie stood amazed for a moment and then obeyed. She began praising God for every possible thing she could praise Him for. She praised God for who He was; she praised Him for what He'd done in times past in her life; and she praised God for all He had done and was doing in her children's lives. She filled the bathroom with praise as she named the many, many blessings and miracles that had already taken place in Meg's journey.

And then, in faith she thanked God for what she believed He was going to do. She just praised Him and continued to praise Him as she finished her shower and got ready for whatever this day might hold. She wiped her swollen eyes and realized that her tears of praise had bathed her broken heart in peace.

"I've got to tell someone," she said. "Praise is what God really wants us to do on this day!"

She decided to call Charlie. Kathie left a message in his mailbox, "Charlie, it's Kathie; the order from the Lord for this Day of Prayer and Fasting is simply *Praise Me!*"

Chapter 15

Am I Dying?

Saturday, April 17

* * * * *

It was close to noon when Shar arrived and realized that Megan was failing quickly.

I know Kathie would want to be here.

She tried to text and call Kathie but got no response. Shar called the front desk of the Ritz and asked to be connected to the bell stand. When Jeremy, one of Megan's friends, answered, Shar said, "Please don't tell the other Ritz staff, but Megan is very bad, and I have to talk with Kathie. She doesn't answer her cell phone or the room phone, and I'm concerned. Please do me a favor and see if she is in the room."

Kathie was not there. Shar and Jeremy didn't know Kathie had turned off her phone to block out all distractions while she was praying. As Kathie walked to her car, she texted Wayne to see if he needed her to pick up anything on the way.

"Just come and drive safely," he texted back.

Kathie was still bathed in peace. She noticed that she'd missed several text messages and calls from Shar but figured she'd see her in fifteen minutes.

Mandi shared Shar's concerns and desperation. She feared that her sister was dying, that the hospital staff would not let them know until the last minute, and her mom was not there.

"She needs to be here...now," Mandi said as she texted her mom.

Kathie's phone beeped as she pulled into the Barnes Parking Garage. The text from Mandi read: "Where are you? Meg is really bad!"

Kathie grabbed her purse and bag and ran into the hospital. When she exited the elevator on the fifth floor, she saw one of Wayne's cousins standing by the ICU door sobbing. Kathie could only think of the worst.

Inside the ICU hallway Kathie saw that her mother was weeping uncontrollably, but Kathie dashed down the long hall to Room #12.

As Kathie approached Megan's bed, she glimpsed her sleeping daughter, and her peace returned. Yes, Meg was very sick; nevertheless, because of her encounter with Almighty God just moments earlier in the Ritz bathroom sanctuary, Kathie would choose to praise her fears away.

Still wondering about Mandi's text message, the sobbing cousin, and her weeping mom, Kathie asked Sharon about Meg's reports from earlier that morning. Assuming that Kathie was aware of the no-hope details, Sharon referred to the "We've waited too long" conversation.

"No! No!" Kathie cried out.

She left the room to look for Wayne.

* * * * *

During the long, lonely nights in March, Megan had dealt with the possibility of her approaching death. Today as she struggled to stay awake, she knew that this must be what it felt like to wait for death to come.

As she lay with her eyes closed, she recalled the peace that enveloped her at home when she surrendered her heart and her life totally into God's care. With that scene emblazoned in her memory, she silently breathed her motto, *Through this, even this day, Lord, I will demonstrate that Christ is enough —come what may!*

Unlike the thoughts about death that Megan faced in the darkness of her own bedroom, today she faced the fear of death that was written on the faces of those who cared for her. She didn't want to die, but she also knew she wasn't afraid to die. She had a peace that she couldn't explain; she knew she was ready to meet Jesus if that was God's will.

But, she thought, *I would like to know: Is today the day?*

Too weak to talk, Megan motioned for her writing tools.

Throughout the day, Megan had appeared unaware of her surroundings and responded only when the medical staff or a family member awakened her, so Kathie was surprised that Megan was initiating communication. She was further dumbfounded that Megan guarded the words from view with her left hand as her frail right hand worked to form the barely legible letters.

Megan decided to show the note to her mom later; she knew her dad would get too emotional. As she finished the note, Megan tore the page from the pad, handed the pad and pen back to her mom, and slipped the note beneath her blanket. The room was busy again while nurses scurried in and out. Megan still clutched the note, waiting for the right moment to give it to Mom. Finally the nurses and Dad left.

Kathie read Megan's scribbles. "Am I dying? Everyone is here. Keep it on the DL."

Wayne reentered before Kathie could answer. Understanding that DL meant to keep Meg's questions on the "down low" and not share them with anyone, she wrote, "No, you're not dying. It's Saturday, and it's easy for everyone to be here."

Kathie was not denying the real possibility that her daughter could die, but neither would she ignore that this was a God-called day of prayer and fasting. She chose to speak praise and embrace hope.

Megan's rising temperature, low blood pressure, and chattering LVAD increased concerns. In a desperate effort to spare Megan's life, the doctor scheduled an emergency in-room procedure to change some of Megan's ports in case they were points of infection. This caring physician knew he had to do something. He ordered that the blood thinning medication be stopped and announced that he would start the procedure as soon as he felt it was safe.

* * * * *

Throughout the entire hospital experience, Megan had shown little fear. She approached everything pragmatically, spiritually, and courageously.

Changing oxygen masks on this day, though, terrified her. Throughout the day Megan had graduated to more sophisticated oxygen masks as her breathing worsened. She had gone from the simple cannula that fit into her nose to the mask with a balloon that covered her nose completely. The next step was a larger, more comprehensive mask, one that would cover her nose and her mouth. She struggled to make the transition.

I'm afraid. I'm so very afraid!

She reasoned that if she could hardly breathe with the current mask, she would not breathe at all until the nurse got the new mask on. Consumed with fear of not being able to breathe, she held on to the smaller mask, afraid to let it go. Only after consistent, patient encouragement did she trust the nurse and allow the transition to the larger mask.

* * * * *

The family began congregating in an empty room near Megan's. It was already sanitized for a new patient, but the medical staff sensed the family's need to stay near Megan. Out-of-town relatives looked at Megan from the hall and then came into the spare room to be comforted. Many times that day, the room provided a private place where family and friends joined hands and hearts in prayer.

* * * * *

At about 2:00 p.m. the medical staff began preparation for the procedure. Wayne was thankful that the nurses had given them the blessing of this large room so the procedure could be done right there.

The surgeon in charge encouraged Wayne, Kathie, and Mandi to remain. With everyone scrubbed and robed, the ten members of the medical team and the three family members took their places. Because of Megan's low weight, and wanting to limit any further complications, the anesthesiologist gave Megan just enough sedation to keep her asleep during what was supposed to be a fifteen-minute procedure.

The surgical sheet was pulled over Megan and the surgeon decided to remove the neck port first, the one that had the most tubes and was most likely to be a point of infection. The old tube came out easily, but the new port refused to go into the vein. Megan began to bleed profusely from the open wound in her neck.

About twenty minutes into the failing procedure, Megan began to stir. Kathie ducked her head under the sheet, and Mandi followed her. Wayne saw the nurse look at the doctor with raised eyebrows as though to say, *"What should we do? This is against the sterile environmental code!"*

The doctor gently responded, "It's okay. Just let them be with her."

Wayne felt the doctor was in so many words saying, *I'm not sure she'll make it anyway. Let them have the peace of knowing they were with her.*

Kathie and Mandi took turns talking quietly. "It's okay, Megan." "Just lay still." "Jesus is with you." "They'll be done soon."

The surgeon and medical staff worked professionally and frantically. Finally the port was in place. Praise God Megan was breathing and had made it through the surgery.

After the nurses removed the surgical sheet, they focused on trying to get the neck wound to stop bleeding. As one nurse held a large piece of gauze over the wound, another nurse attempted to tape it; but before she could secure the tape, the gauze was saturated with blood. They tried again and again.

Finally one nurse left the room to request a five-pound sandbag. While other nurses held pressure on the wound, she kept checking the pneumatic tube that was supposed to carry the life-saving bag to her floor. Finally she left the unit and ran the long trek through the hospital to personally retrieve the sandbag. She knew her patient needed it, and needed it now.

Seeing the desperateness of the situation, Wayne sent a plea for prayer.

• 3:00 p.m. Had to do emergency procedure. Having a difficult time stopping the bleeding. Trouble during the procedure and Meg woke. We are definitely praying for God's miraculous touch today.

Wayne looked up from his computer to see the nurse return. She applied the heavy sandbag to Megan's neck on top of the blood-saturated gauze. Although some blood continued to trickle down Megan's neck onto her sheet, the bleeding began to slow.

Wayne, Kathie, and Mandi needed a brief break, so Shar offered to stay with Meg. Since Meg was too weak to talk, Shar began to sing a song that pointed out that God is working even when we can't see Him in action.

She realized someone had walked into the room and was standing behind her. She turned and found herself face to face with a doctor. Although she was embarrassed, she gently poked the doctor's chest and continued singing, "God is working even now."

The doctor smiled, checked Megan, and left the room without a word.

Chapter 16

God's Children Praying

Saturday, April 17

* * * * *

On Saturday, just past noon, as Megan struggled to breathe and the Moss family wondered if they were at the end of the story, the Missouri District Children's Bible Quizzing was still in progress at the Church of the Nazarene in Mexico, Missouri, which was Kathie's home church.

Several of the adults had been multitasking that day: watching the quiz and their phones. Some knew Megan, and others knew her need because their churches were praying for her.

When one of those adults, Cheri, recognized the severity of Megan's dilemma, she asked the quiz director if they could pray for Megan at the end of the award ceremony. The director agreed.

The more Cheri thought about praying for Megan, the more she sensed that God wanted the children to pray. If the children prayed, they would take an active part in what God was doing. She believed that God could use this to transfer deep faith to these little ones as they prayed, expecting God to answer.

When the award ceremony ended, in words she thought second through sixth graders could understand, Cheri told about Megan's need for a heart and explained what it meant to intercede for someone.

"Megan is on the waiting list for a heart, but now she has an infection that has made her too sick to receive a heart." Cheri closed with clear words of direction, "I want you to ask God for two things: number one, ask Him to take away all of Megan's infection; and number two, ask Him to find a heart because the doctors say tomorrow is the deadline."

Realizing that children understand best with visual associations, Cheri asked the children from the Ferguson Church to come stand at the altar.

"These children from Megan's church will *be* Megan," she said. "Now, I want all the rest of you children, your parents, and other adults to gather around the Ferguson children, lay hands on them, and we will intercede for Megan."

"I would like the children to pray first. As each child prays aloud, the rest of us will agree together with each prayer. Once the children are finished, the adults may pray if they care to." They bowed their heads, and without further encouragement, the children began praying aloud.

After the children and several adults prayed, God's Spirit was close. Cheri was sure she'd never seen children pray so earnestly and cry so many tears before the Lord. It seemed evident that the sincere, earnest prayers of these children did indeed ascend to heaven as a fragrant offering of intercession before the Lord.

Along with their colorful ribbons, these children took their faith in God and belief in prayer back to their home churches and church prayer chains. Faith was being transferred.

* * * * *

Around 2:00 p.m. Sharon called her husband, Richard, to update him on Megan's failing condition and the emergency procedure. Richard had prayed for Megan all morning but wondered if the family should accept what appeared to be inevitable.

We have great faith in what God can do, he thought, *but there comes a time when we must yield to God's will even when it isn't what we want.*

Richard returned to his recliner and read the scripture portion for the day. In Deuteronomy 9 God was angry with the stubborn, complaining Israelites and was ready to destroy them. In loving protest, Moses begged God to spare them for the sake of the people he loved, but also because he was afraid the unbelieving Egyptians would think that his God was unable "to bring them to the land that he had promised" (Deuteronomy 9:28).

Richard thought of the waiting room witness as well as the hundreds of emails that had come from all over the world. Because of technology, it seemed that *everybody* had heard about Megan. Richard began to wonder what the skeptics and unbelievers would think if God let Megan die.

Along with many other blog followers who read the desperate 3:00 p.m. call to prayer, Richard decided to intensify his praying and fortify his faith.

* * * * *

It was almost 3:00 p.m. when Josh's dorm room phone rang at MidAmerica Nazarene University. His sobbing mom, Sheryl, informed him that the doctors weren't sure his cousin Megan would make it. Megan had pneumonia and was so weak that, even if a donor heart became available, she was too sick to receive it. Josh's stomach sank.

"Josh, pray!" his mom instructed.

From Josh's window he saw Cook Gymnasium. God reminded him that in that building were more than 1,000 high school students from seven states who had gathered for MAX (MidAmerica Xtreme), three days of competition in Bible quizzing, sports, art, and music. He was sure they were nearing the end of the award ceremony so he left his room and sprinted toward Cook.

He decided to go through a back entrance where he knew he would find an administrator. The first person he saw was Dr. Ed Robinson, the university president.

"We need to pray for my cousin," Josh told him. Dr. Robinson encouraged Josh to get the attention of one of the event leaders because the ceremony would end soon.

Josh spotted Greg Gilberto, one of the people in charge, standing backstage and told him, "I just got a message from my mom; my 23-year-old cousin is dying. I would like us to pray for her."

Greg knew Josh and respected this young man's strong faith. Nevertheless, Greg also was responsible to maintain a tight schedule. These 1,000 kids and their parents had miles to go to get home that night. While Josh stood waiting, Greg prayed. He sensed God saying, *"Yes, you need to let Josh pray for his cousin!"*

So at the end, the emcee announced, "Josh Dampf, the MidAmerica Nazarene University Student Body President, will close our ceremony in prayer."

Josh decided that before he prayed he needed to help this group of teens know what it meant to intercede and pray in unity.

"Just like you, I grew up coming to this competition each year," Josh began. "My 23-year-old cousin, Megan, also grew up participating in MAX, but today she is very sick and needs a donor heart."

He told some of the details and the reason for the immediate need for prayer. He explained why he believed God could heal his cousin and why the Lord is known as the Great Physician.

Josh then felt impressed to tell the miracle story of his Aunt Shar, his mom's younger sister. "All my life, I've heard my mom tell the story of how my Aunt Shar was brought back to life by prayer when she was a toddler."

He described that his mom was almost five years old when her family attended a denominational assembly in Portland, Oregon. While running down a ramp, his Aunt Shar had fallen over the edge—30 feet to the concrete floor. Her body went limp and her eyes rolled back in her head; the convention nurse told the family, "I'm sorry, but she is dead."

Josh continued, "My grandma and grandpa didn't accept the bleak report. Instead, they sped to the nearest hospital. Someone who believed in miracles interrupted an important convention and asked ten thousand people to intercede for the toddler who had fallen to her death. While the people were praying, my grandparents heard noises coming from Shar's throat. She began to breathe!

"The little girl who left the convention center with no pulse *walked* out of that emergency room with no injuries—not even a broken bone!—because a group of people were willing to intercede and believe for a miracle for a little girl they didn't even know.

"Without a miracle, Megan will die today! I believe in a God who can do the impossible when His people intercede! What is intercession? It's when you have proactive faith and choose to stand in the gap; you take the burden of prayer for someone who cannot pray for herself."

In closing Josh explained, "I don't believe God simply gives us whatever we ask for. Yet I do believe God wants to reveal Himself to His people. If God does not heal Megan, I *know* my family will continue to proclaim His faithfulness. But I also know that if Megan is healed, thousands of people just like you and me will see their God as a healer. Think of the renewal God could bring to the churches represented in this gymnasium today if each of us saw God as a healer, a God of miracles, a God who is *real*."

Josh knew he needed to say one more thing. "I've heard stories of miracles from my parents and grandparents, and I have always wondered why their experience with God seemed so different from mine. I believe in my heart today, however, that God is the same yesterday, today and forever, and I am asking you to join with me in intercession.

"Right now we need to specifically pray about the pneumonia in Megan's body. The doctors say that if this pneumonia doesn't leave, she has no hope for a transplant. Let's pray."

Josh began pacing and praying. Teens, parents, and college students who didn't even know Megan began praying so fervently that some even wept.

As Josh ended his prayer, it seemed that he heard God say, *I've heard you, child. I will answer.*

When Josh finished praying, the energetic group simply sat soaking in the presence of God that permeated the auditorium.

As Josh walked off the stage, he thought about the fact that his mom, grandma, and aunts had been praying since the fall 2009 Come to the Fire Conference that their faith would be transferred to the next generation.

Our generation is going to see our own miracle! he decided, a thought that was echoed by hundreds of MAX participants who were on their way home.

At about 5:00 p.m., Megan opened her eyes and motioned for her paper and pen.

"How am I supposed to eat and drink with this thing on?" she wrote, referring to her large mask.

Megan hadn't asked for food in weeks. Her shocked mother replied, "Megan, you can eat and drink whenever you're ready. I'll pull the mask back and slip food in. Just let me know when you're ready."

Megan pulled the mask back and quickly whispered, "I'm ready."

Her mom called for Gina, the nurse, and asked if Megan could have some pudding and juice. Equally stunned that this *dying* girl was asking for food, Gina said, "Of course, I'll get her something to eat."

In minutes the nurse returned to an eager eater. Megan even helped pull her mask back. She quickly consumed almost two-thirds of the bowl of pudding and drank some apple juice.

This is miraculous! Kathie thought.

* * * * *

Megan's room was again a flurry of activity, but now all the faces were smiling. The medical staff and family realized that they were watching the unbelievable happen. It had to be supernatural because Megan's improvement wasn't medically possible.

Chapter 17

I Want to Sign

Saturday, April 17

* * * * *

Due to Megan's weakened condition and the
need to keep her room as germ-free as possible, the
family announced that Megan would have no non-
family visitors that night. Jason, Dani, Mandi, and
Kyle spent the evening with Megan while Wayne,
Kathie and the other family members visited with
the many guests in the waiting room.

Occasionally Wayne and Kathie checked on
Meg, and each time they were relieved to discover
that their girl was showing improvement. Megan
even held a lengthy conversation with her brother,
Jason, by writing notes to him.

At 9:00 p.m. Wayne and Kathie left the waiting
room friends and returned to Megan's room, where

her siblings and their spouses were leaving. Jason and Dani had a long trip ahead of them, and Mandi and Kyle needed to get Kinsley, who had been at the sitter's all day. Since he'd hardly seen his kids, Wayne walked Jason and Dani to the elevator. Then Wayne returned to the waiting room to socialize with the few remaining family members.

Just as Wayne sat down, he saw Kathie at the door. She mouthed: "Come. Quick."

Wayne thought the worst. He jumped up, hurried out of the waiting room, and met her in the hall.

"Megan's okay!" Kathie quickly reassured him. "The nurse got a call a few minutes ago. We might have a heart. She told me she had good news and bad news: the bad news is Megan can't eat or drink anything; the good news is that they might have a donor heart that is a match."

Wayne knew he should be jumping with joy, but the events of the day and his conversation with Dr. Wang that morning kept replaying. Wayne wanted to be excited, but he cautiously asked, "Does Dr. Wang think she's strong enough?"

"We haven't talked to any doctors, but the nurse said Megan's fever is gone, her white blood count is coming down, her lungs are clear, and the bleeding has stopped," Kathie answered.

This report was unbelievable, except they had been praying for a real, faith-changing miracle. Kathie continued, "The doctors must feel she can handle the surgery."

When Wayne and Kathie learned that they would have a two-hour wait before they knew if the heart was a match, they decided, "Let's tell only the people in the waiting room and have them promise to keep our secret. Just tell the blog readers to keep praying that the infection will be completely gone, just in case..."

As soon as Mandi heard the good news, she called Jason and Dani and caught them before they left the parking garage. They headed back up to 56ICU.

When most of the visitors were gone and the few remaining family members were deciding to call it a day, a large group of new guests arrived. Children and teens from North County Christian School had played a ballgame at Forest Park and wanted to see how Megan was doing before they headed home. When Wayne returned to the waiting room to share the secret, the waiting room was full of the next generation.

Wayne called the family and close friends into the kitchenette. His wide smile almost gave away the secret.

"You have to promise to keep this a secret. Promise me you won't put it on Facebook," he said with a laugh.

Everyone nodded.

"We have the possibility of a heart." The group erupted into praise. "But remember, it's not for sure, so don't tell anyone! Just pray that the heart will be a perfect match, and that Megan's infection will totally disappear."

The group of children, teens, and adults joined hands as Wayne led them in a prayer of thanksgiving; and then he prayed for God's comfort to surround the donor's family.

Most participants in this circle were younger than sixteen, and Sheryl believed that God had brought them there to experience a faith-establishing moment. When Wayne said the "Amen," Sheryl told the youngsters, "Remember, God chose you to be here tonight to hear this special news. Keep praying because you will see a miracle!"

At 9:30 p.m. Wayne said good-bye to the few remaining visitors and entered the door to ICU. At the room, a smiling Dr. Ewald and an alert Megan greeted him.

"We have a perfect heart, and I have accepted it on your behalf," Dr. Ewald told Megan. "If you want it, I will need you to sign the paperwork."

Want it? Megan thought. *Of course I want it!*

Megan immediately made the scribbling sign with her right hand. Since she still had the massive oxygen mask on, her mom thought she was asking for paper and pen to write them a note. When Mom handed her the notepad, Megan pulled her mask back and quietly but confidently whispered, "I want to sign."

Dr. Ewald reviewed the consent form and showed Megan where to sign. The doctor and Megan embraced while Mom photographed this moment.

It was 9:30 p.m. in St. Louis, but 7:30 p.m. and the end of the Day of Prayer and Fasting on the West Coast. During the hours of this day, Megan had gone from too sick to even think of receiving a transplant to being strong enough to sign the transplant consent form. God heard the prayers of

His children and gave them a faith-transferring miracle.

Jason and Dani hurried home to get sleeping bags and pillows so they could spend the night at the hospital. Mandi and Kyle called the sitters and arranged for thirteen-month old Kinsley to spend her first night away from her mommy and daddy.

Wayne returned to the waiting room and told the family and friends who were still there, "We have a heart. God has given us a miracle."

This time tears of joy were mixed with hugs and praise to the King of kings and Lord of lords. Wayne gave everyone permission to let the world know the good news.

It seemed very fitting to end this eventful day that had gone from the darkest morning to the brightest night by singing the Doxology. This happy-hearted daddy led the group in singing, "Praise God from whom all blessings flow. Praise Him all creatures here below. Praise Him above ye heavenly host. Praise Father, Son, and Holy Ghost. Amen!"

The brink of disaster and the brink of a miracle were at the same point, and God in His mercy gave Megan, her praying friends, and the watching world a real miracle.

Kathie was instantly on her laptop updating her Facebook friends. The rest of the family had grabbed their technology toys. Mouths and thumbs were sending the message quickly, and those who received the good news passed it on to their friends, families, and churches. Within minutes the news, "We have a heart!" had made it around the world.

Much like the night before Easter, two weeks earlier, each family member had a decision to make. Should they be at the hospital for Megan's surgery or go to church? Megan's immediate family would be at the hospital, along with Aunt Sharon. The others would go to church and participate in the rest of the miracle—celebrating God's faithfulness.

It was nearing 11:00 p.m., and Sharon, Sheryl, and Wayne were still in the waiting room talking; Kathie decided to stay with them while the nurse gave Megan her pre-op bath. Kathie grabbed her Bible and said, "I just have to share the scripture that the Lord led me to this morning."

As she was finding the passage, she said, "One of the most incredible things about these last several months is how God has used His Word to provide comfort, to give direction, and to strengthen our faith. Here, listen to this from 2 Corinthians 1:3-11 in the New Living Translation:

"'All praise to God the Father of our Lord Jesus Christ...He comforts us in all our troubles so that we can comfort others...We were crushed and overwhelmed beyond our ability to endure, and we thought we would never live through it. In fact, we expected to die. But as a result, we stopped relying on ourselves and learned to rely only on God, who raises the dead. And he did rescue us from mortal danger, and he will rescue us again...Then many people will give thanks because God has graciously answered so many prayers for our safety.'"

By the time Kathie finished reading, the group had exhausted their stash of tissues and were convinced that Meg had been kept safe by the prayers of so many people. Between their tears, they saw a friend come from the elevator. Sheryl exclaimed, "Jill, it's almost midnight!"

"I know, but I couldn't sleep after I got the message. I figured I could have my own prayer vigil while the rest of you slept. I just want you to know that you can rest because someone is praying."

Kathie and Wayne had received numerous Facebook posts since the ten o'clock blog indicating that many friends planned to pray instead of sleep. Jill became a visible reminder that friends were staying up all night, all over the world, praying for the rest of God's miracle.

Since the sleeping bag and pillow were still in the back of Wayne's van, he decided to stay in the parking garage so he'd be on the spot until Sharon called him before the surgery.

As Wayne settled, he tried to keep his thoughts positive, but he couldn't help but remember what the doctors had said, "The receipt of a heart is never a sure thing until it arrives."

Wayne knew if the recovery surgeon found any other diseased organ in the donor, then the donation would be cancelled. In the darkness of his van with only the quiet hum of the garage exhaust fan, Wayne laid his fears at Jesus' feet and promptly fell asleep.

Megan's nurse, Courtney, received a call from the doctor. There would be a delay while the transplant organization tried to find a recipient for the donor's lungs.

"That's fine," Kathie said. "That will give Megan a few more hours to get stronger and will give us a few more hours of sleep."

Kathie settled in the recliner by Meg's bed, and Sharon made her bed in Consult Room #2. She wrote in her journal, "What an incredible day! Within a span of 12 hours, the exact hours of the fast, we went from heaviness and weeping to exhilaration and rejoicing. Thank you, God, for this miracle!"

* * * * *

Throughout that day multiple medical teams were busy coordinating efforts to bring Megan's miracle closer to completion.

Chapter 18

God's Incredible View

Saturday, April 17 – Sunday, April 18

* * * * *

When the nursing staff walked into Megan's room that Saturday, they obviously had heavy spirits. It was especially difficult for Gina, Megan's assigned nurse. She grieved as more and more signs indicated that Megan was too unstable to receive a transplant even if a heart became available.

Gina's own heart was breaking, not only for this beautiful girl, but also for each of the family members who clearly loved her so much. Every time Gina charted a weakening vital sign or received results of worsening blood work, her heart ached more deeply. As much as Gina and her co-workers tried to hide their disappointment, Gina knew Megan's father could sense their concern. She also knew he responded by praying more fervently.

The discouraged staff marveled at the amazing, positive spirit of Megan and her family. It was protocol for a nurse to remain calm and positive, but Gina rarely saw those qualities displayed in a family during trauma. As Megan's breathing became more difficult, Megan's anxiety level rose. Gina knew she was witnessing a rare, beautiful scene as she watched Megan's mom and sister calm Megan.

Throughout the morning and early afternoon hours, Gina watched helplessly as Megan's condition spiraled downward. Her white blood count was up, and her respiratory status was diminishing. After the bedside procedure, Megan was losing blood from an old central line site that would not clot. With Megan's excessive blood loss, the nurses were sure the increased risks had sealed Megan's doom.

During the mid-afternoon hours, Dr. Wang notified the ICU team that there was a potential heart available for Megan. Unfortunately, Megan was so sick he wasn't sure he could safely perform the surgery.

The team debated whether or not Megan needed to be placed on respiratory life-support. They considered whether or not the pneumonia was severe enough that *it* would take her life on this day.

"What would it take to turn Megan around in time to get this heart?" they asked.

The consensus was: "It would take a miracle!"

At about 5:00 p.m., an amazing thing happened. Megan asked for food. Gina knew Megan had refused food for days. *This is unbelievable; no one this sick asks for food.*

Almost simultaneously, Dr. Wang called and said, "Please request one more lab test to see if Megan's white blood count shows any sign of decreasing."

Gina ordered the blood work and thought, "Megan's life literally depends on the results of this one test."

For Gina, time seemed to stand still until the results came back. To everyone's disbelief, the white blood count had improved! The ICU team started to feel hope. When Gina called Dr. Wang, he confirmed that Megan had improved enough to make her eligible for the transplant.

During the next hour, Gina watched in disbelief as Megan appeared to get better by the moment. As Megan began to look more alert, Gina wanted to tell the family her secret about the heart, but knew she couldn't. So she just kept praying, "God, help Megan get better!"

At 7:00 p.m. Gina's shift ended and she updated Courtney on the dilemma-filled day. She told the new caregiver how the morning had spiraled into a scary and saddening afternoon but how the sad, hopeless afternoon had somehow led into a hopeful evening. Gina shared the good news about the possibility of the heart but reminded Courtney that it was a secret since they were still waiting on the cardiologist's report on the donor heart.

Throughout the evening Gina called the ICU desk to get updates and checked the blog written by Megan's dad. She had to know if she had witnessed a miracle, and if so, how it was going to end.

Gina continued to pray believing that Megan would get a second chance at life. She also believed that the family's faith would continue to resound and that they would become public voices to encourage organ donation.

* * * * *

It was 3:45 p.m. and Brian Scheller, a nurse at the Mid-America Transplant Services, was hurrying to get his family to Saturday Mass. As the house door closed behind him, his pager beeped. Brian asked his wife to drive so he could call his office.

"We have a heart that might be a match for Megan Moss," he was told.

At this point, Megan was a backup for the heart. One person was ahead of her, but that patient's doctor had not made a decision yet.

Brian called Dr. Ewald who was at his daughter's baseball game. Dr. Ewald agreed to look at the donor information on his computer and get back with Brian. Within a brief time, Dr. Ewald confirmed that the heart was a match. Even though he knew it would take a miracle for Megan Moss to be well enough to receive this heart, he instructed Brian to call the donor coordinator, express their interest in the heart, and request a cardiac catherization to make sure the heart was free of any coronary artery disease.

Dr. Ewald told Brian that as soon as the game was over, he would call Barnes about the possibility of a heart for Megan.

While his family went into church, Brian called the transplant organization. The person responded, "We're sorry, but someone else is ahead of Megan on the list, and we haven't been able to find a doctor available today to do a heart catherization."

"Our patient can't live much longer without a heart," Brian explained insistently. "If for some reason the other patient can't receive this donor heart, it is critical that you do everything possible to find a cardiologist to do this procedure so I can know whether or not it is a perfect match for our patient. Please, please make one more call."

The person at the organization agreed to make one more call.

Brian continued to think about this 23-year-old girl who waited in Barnes hospital. This was the closest they'd come to offering her life. He could certainly understand the transplant organization's dilemma, but he believed in prayer and miracles.

He joined his family in Mass while praying and watching his beeper for good news. Within a short while, his pager vibrated. It was a miracle! The donor coordinator reported that the *one* more phone call had been successful. He had found a cardiologist who was willing to do the test and was on his way to the cath lab.

Thank you, God! Brian thought. Brian realized that Megan was still in back-up status, but since one miracle had happened, maybe another one could, too.

An hour later, the miracle call came from the donor coordinator: the cath test was done and negative for heart disease, and the other patient was not a good match. Megan was at the top of the list. Brian called Dr. Ewald with the good news.

Now it was Brian's job to coordinate the receipt of this precious organ. After requesting the heart for Megan, he called the transplant coordinator at Barnes so their team could plan for the heart and prep Megan for surgery.

Brian then scheduled the jet, the ambulance, and the helicopter that would be necessary to make this time-critical transplant happen. He knew a donor heart could remain on ice for only four to six hours. The heart was in Texas and since Missouri and Texas are not near neighbors, Brian knew the timing of every part of his plan had to be exact.

The surgery to recover the heart would occur during the night. Brian established the timeline and then called the transplant coordinator at Barnes. This coordinator then called the recovering surgeons and arranged for them to meet Brian at the Spirit of St. Louis Airport.

Both hospitals had originally hoped for a 2:00 a.m. surgery, but Brian received a call from the out-of-state transplant organization indicating that they couldn't find a recipient for the donor lungs. The recovery operating room time would have to be delayed. A few hours later Brian received another call from the donor coordinator; a recipient was found for the lungs, and Megan's surgery could be scheduled.

Brian and the accompanying surgeons boarded a jet at the Spirit of St. Louis airport at about 3:00

a.m. Once at the hospital in Texas, the recovering surgeons checked all donor information, including test results. Then they thoroughly examined the heart; it was not only healthy but also was the exact size and match that Megan needed.

It was perfect!

Brian called the transplant coordinator at Barnes to communicate the news and review the timeline.

The recovery surgeons gave the go ahead for the heart retrieval and the surgery began. From his vantage point in the operating room, Brian called Barnes to start Megan's surgery.

While Brian witnessed the recovery surgery, he repeatedly called the operating room coordinator at Barnes. Together they made sure all of the time-sensitive checkpoints of the recovery surgery in Texas were coordinated perfectly with what was taking place in St. Louis. Megan's defibrillator could now be surgically removed, and Dr. Wang could prepare Megan's chest cavity to receive her new heart.

After the successful retrieval, Brian helped package the donor heart for transport. Brian and the surgeons bounded for the waiting ambulance carrying the special ice case that held life for Megan Moss. The time this precious cargo could be without blood flow was limited and every minute counted.

Once in the ambulance, Brian made three important phone calls. First he called the pilot of their jet and told him, "Start the engines. We're on our way."

Next he called the transplant coordinator at Barnes to let him know the expected arrival time. And then he called the helicopter pilot in St. Louis who would be on the runway at the expected landing time.

As the jet landed and the recovery surgeons boarded the helicopter, Brian made his final phone call to Barnes. "We landed and the helicopter is on its way."

During Brian's career he had participated in many organ retrievals, but he knew the coordination and timing of this heart for Megan Moss was not only amazing—it was miraculous.

Chapter 19

Just Say, "Jesus"

Sunday, April 18

* * * * *

Through the early morning hours, Megan's stats continued to improve, and she became more alert and able to anticipate the surgery. She had been too sick to anticipate the LVAD surgery, but now she had a scar on her chest to remind her that her breastbone would have to be sawed open again to receive her new heart. She couldn't sleep so neither did her mom.

When Wayne received his wake-up call in the van at 4:30 a.m., he thought of the update he wanted to give his friends who had prayed through the night:

4:40 a.m. Prep is scheduled for 5:30 a.m. and surgery about an hour later. It should take 4-6 hours. Meg will be in an induced sleep for two days after surgery. She is anxious: pray for peace and comfort and that Jesus will hold her. God is awesome!

* * * * *

Shortly before 5:00 a.m., Megan's anxiety increased. She couldn't stop visualizing the surgery. Since she had already experienced a chemically induced sleep, she became even more anxious as she anticipated the scary awakening and nightmarish days that could follow. She also knew what post-operative pain would be like.

Last but not least, it was uncomfortable knowing that you were not only being kept alive by machines during induced sleep, but you depended on others to care for your every need. What a humbling, scary place to be. Megan's legs and arms shook, and her heart rate soared.

When Megan's apprehension affected her breathing, the nurse had an idea.

"Megan, I need you to take slow, deep breaths," Courtney instructed. "Just say what I say. Breathe in saying, 'Jeeeee' and breathe out saying, '-sus.'"

Megan did her best but couldn't slow her breathing enough to speak the syllables.

Courtney continued, "Good try, Megan! Try again. Just say, 'Je-----sus.' He's helping you, Megan. Keep saying His name."

It wasn't magic, and it wasn't listed in the nursing manuals, but it worked. Courtney sang, "Jesus loves me, this I know, for the Bible tells me so. Little ones to Him belong; they are weak, but He is strong."

177

At 5:30 a.m. Courtney updated the family. Everything was going well. The heart would be in transit soon and Megan would be transferred to the operating room shortly.

It was close to 6:00 a.m. when Courtney gave the "We're ready" signal.

Dr. Wang, the transplant surgeon, led the procession of doctors and nurses who wheeled Megan and all of her life-supporting equipment down the hall to the waiting elevator. Family and friends said words of love and promised prayers as Megan rode by.

"Remember, you're all covered with prayer," Kathie called to the medical staff.

The elevator door closed.

This was a sacred moment that called for worship. Pastor Caddy led the group in a prayer of thanksgiving. And then in grateful praise, Wayne led the participants in "The Doxology." This daddy's weeping had turned to praise as he recognized God's miracle that had brought them to this place.

Someone remembered that it was Kathie's birthday and sang "Happy Birthday" to her. That was the earliest and sweetest birthday serenade Kathie had ever received, and it was certainly destined to be the most memorable.

Since at least an hour would pass before the operating room (OR) nurse called the waiting room with the promised updates, the family went to the cafeteria for breakfast. David, one of Megan's nurses, showed up in his street clothes with three large white boxes.

"I was off yesterday, and I'm off today, but I read on the blog last night that Megan got a heart," he explained. "I brought some donuts."

The family welcomed David and the donuts. As Kathie watched Wayne and David talk she thought, *God sure has given us dedicated, caring nurses.*

David looked at his watch and said, "I need to hurry since I made plans to go to church with my mom today."

As he stood, Wayne shook his hand and said, "David, it means so much that you came on your day off. God bless!"

* * * * *

The family returned from the cafeteria at 7:00 a.m. just as the phone rang. The nurse said, "This is your first call from OR. We are beginning Megan's surgery, and she is doing fine. The first step will be to remove the defibrillator."

The family visited until the phone rang again at 8:00 a.m. when the nurse reported, "This is your hourly update. All is going well."

The family was slightly apprehensive when the phone didn't ring right at nine, so when it rang at 9:12 a.m., everyone stopped talking and watched Wayne for any indication of concern. They sighed when they saw him smile and say, "Thanks! We'll continue praying!"

The defibrillator had been removed successfully. The donor heart had just arrived, and the surgeons were ready to place it in Megan.

At 10:15 a.m. there was another phone call from the OR. The transplant surgery was still in progress, and although they were dealing with some bleeding, all was well. Wayne wrote a blog update in case anyone was checking.

- 10:15 a.m. Megan's new heart is being implanted. Pray for guidance of the surgeon's hands, for controlled bleeding, and for God's arm to be around Megan.

At 11:26 a.m. the phone rang again.

"We have a beating heart!"

By this time most worship services across the nation were in progress, but Wayne wanted phone followers to know the news:

- 11:35 a.m. Megan has a new beating heart. To God be the glory; great things He has done.

* * * * *

When Joyce left her job as unit secretary in 56ICU on Friday, she doubted that Megan Moss would be alive when she returned to work on Monday. Although she knew Megan only as a patient, she had prayed earnestly for her all weekend. Unaware of recent blog posts and answers to prayer, Joyce went to Sunday morning worship with a heavy heart.

As was the custom in Joyce's church, fellow believers prayed aloud while the pastor led in prayer, and Joyce was eager to take her petition for Megan to the Lord. With hands raised and tears flowing, she prayed, "Oh, God, provide a heart for Megan. This girl needs a heart. Megan needs a miracle. Oh, God ..."

Who is touching me, Joyce wondered, *and especially during prayer?*

It was a lady down the row from her; not only was she listening to the pastor, praying her own prayer, and listening to Joyce, she was following the blog via her phone. This lady didn't know Megan but pointed to her phone and told Joyce, "Megan just got her heart, and it is beating!"

The two praised the Lord together.

* * * * *

Since the Ferguson Church of the Nazarene was Megan's home church, the congregation was definitely preoccupied with what was happening at Barnes. Megan's grandpa, Udell Moss, had started this church and had been its pastor for 31 years.

Aware that many of the people in this sanctuary had participated in Megan's miracle by attending the prayer vigil on Friday and by fasting and praying for her all day Saturday, Pastor Caddy pointed to his phone when he came to the pulpit. He encouraged everyone to keep their phones on and make Megan's miracle a priority in their praying as he spoke.

When the pastor dismissed the children for Children's Church, Nancy, who didn't know the Moss women's burden to transfer their faith to the next generation, stood and said, "Please bring the children back; I feel that these children need to experience what is going to take place here today."

The children's workers were surprised, but returned the children to the sanctuary.

While the children found their parents, Darrell, a quiet gentleman, asked if he could speak. Darrell told how God had been teaching him through his praying for Megan that God doesn't perform a miracle when He finally gets a quota of people to pray. Neither does He listen to our prayers so *He* can learn from us and therefore have more options that are available to Him. Darrell said, "I've come to believe that God requires our praying for the sake of our participation and His desire to strengthen *us* as we speak our faith."

Doris Moss, Megan's 82-year-old grandma, stood and said, "I appreciate your prayers for Megan, and I am grateful that God has answered your prayers and given Megan a new heart. But the burden of my heart today is that God will use this miracle to help many people understand their need to let Jesus give them a spiritual heart transplant.

"You may be burdened by sin and think that a good life in Christ is impossible; but it's not impossible with a new heart! You may be brokenhearted by the hurts of your past and your heart is filled with bitterness; you can ask Jesus to give you a new heart, and He will help you forgive and love those who have hurt you. Don't wait until a better time. Accept Jesus today. He's the donor who gave His life for you!"

After she sat, Mom Moss whispered to her daughter Shar, "We need to do a victory march."

Back in the 1960s when this congregation was seeing weekly miracles, they often formed a circle around the sanctuary and walked, singing songs of praise to the Miracle Giver. Shar remembered these marches, but she realized that most people didn't.

"Mom, they don't know what a victory march is," Shar whispered. "But you lead the way, and I'll follow."

The other remnants from the '60s joined the march, and soon others followed. They felt the

Spirit of God as they walked, spoke words of praise, and sang songs of faith.

As everyone returned to his or her seats, Sheryl walked to the microphone.

"What many of you don't know is that my family and friends who went to the Come to the Fire Conference have been praying since November that God would help us successfully transfer our faith to the next generation. Knowing that it was the miracles of the '60s that solidified our faith and kept my siblings and me faithful to the Lord through our teen years, our college years, and the many trials of adult life, we believed that our children needed to see a miracle in their generation."

Sheryl explained, "During the exact time that Megan was dying yesterday, people around the world were praying and fasting, and children at the Missouri District Quiz and teens at MAX were interceding. At both the quiz and at MAX, children and teens were spontaneously learning what it means to intercede. Then these children and teens prayed, they believed, and God gave us a miracle. I'd say that God has answered our prayer and has helped us transfer our faith to the next generation. These children and teens will never forget that *they* prayed, and God spared Megan's life in answer to *their* prayers."

As Sheryl finished her sentence, she saw her sister Shar reading her phone. Shar jumped to her feet. "The heart is beating!"

Some sat and cried while others laughed, hugged their friends, and praised God. The joy of the Lord was abundant in that place.

In the midst of Sheryl's rejoicing, she thought of the donor family who was preparing a funeral. She also thought of Jennifer, a young adult who had been in the hospital since December and still needed a heart. She visualized all of the hurting people in the waiting room who waited for news regarding their loved ones.

In the midst of our miracle, we can't forget those who still need comfort, she thought.

Still in a spirit of praise, but with words that brought everyone back to the point of the miracle and their mission, Sheryl prayed for all of the caretakers and medical staff, that they would see God's hand in this miracle. She prayed for the people in the waiting room and the people that Megan's situation had touched around the world, that they would see God as a compassionate Savior and yield their lives to Him. She prayed for Jennifer. And then Sheryl prayed for the donor's family, that God's grace would sustain them and bless them for allowing good to come from their tragedy.

* * * * *

Kathie's Facebook page was full of birthday messages that day. Many from all around the world spoke specifically of the revival God had begun in their hearts because of the concentrated prayer over the last several days.

Kathie also received confirmation that faith was being transferred to the next generation when she read the post from her friend, Jill, who described her daughter's reaction to the worship service at Ferguson Nazarene: "Bella has talked all day about the awesome praise service today. She is so excited that she got to march around the sanctuary in a *holy march* and sing songs. Praise God our children are seeing this miracle and rejoicing!"

Already the Moss family was hearing reports on how God had ignited revival in homes, churches, on college campuses, and beyond. The impact of Megan's miracle was mind-boggling.

Chapter 20

Wrestling with
Possibilities

Sunday, April 18

* * * * *

Megan was still in recovery when the waiting
room phone rang. Someone from Channel 4
wanted to speak with Wayne.

"They sure don't waste time," he said.

His intuition was right; they wanted another
interview that afternoon. The reporter asked Wayne
and Kathie to meet the crew in Forest Park directly
across the street. Wayne agreed.

Within minutes, the phone rang again; Channel
5 also wanted an interview. Wayne explained, "I
already made plans to meet Channel 4 in Forest
Park."

The Channel 5 reporter assured Wayne that he
would work out the details with the other network.

The family could understand their churches
and their friends making a big deal out of Megan's

story, but it was still difficult to believe that the community was this interested.

At the appointed time, Wayne and Kathie walked toward Forest Park and the vans, equipment, and crews from both TV stations. Wayne and Kathie publicly thanked the awesome staff at Barnes for their skill and care. They also thanked the donor family and encouraged viewers to consider being organ donors. Last and best, they credited God for the incredible turnaround in Megan's health that was a last-minute miracle.

* * * * *

While Megan was being transported from recovery to her room, Dr. Wang went to the waiting room to give the family a comprehensive, post-operative report.

"I have good news and bad news," he somberly reported.

The good news: since multiple chest x-rays are taken daily, he never asks for another one just before surgery; he merely uses the most recent one. Today he felt impressed to request another x-ray and saw a blood clot in the aorta in the very place where he usually makes the incision. With the new x-ray information, he adjusted his plan and cut higher so he could miss the clot.

The bad news: although Dr. Wang approached the clot carefully and thought he missed it, he wouldn't know for sure until Megan awakened in two to three days.

"There is always a possibility that I could have snipped a clot and a part of it could have gone to the brain and caused a stroke during the surgery."

Those words hit the hearts of the family like a close-range stun gun, but the doctor wasn't finished. He had also found a blood clot in the damaged left ventricle of Megan's old heart.

Dr. Wang didn't think Megan had suffered a stroke during surgery, but he felt he needed to warn them so they would be prepared for the worst. His parting words were, "Your God answered your prayers."

"Yes, God did answer our prayers, and thank you for being honest with us." Wayne's reply to Dr. Wang was calm, but his insides screamed.

The listening family tried to make sense of all that they had heard. They couldn't imagine why God would want Megan's miracle to end with a stroke, but they chose not to question Him. God had obviously spared Megan from several things that could have taken her life during these last few days. And He had overcome numerous obstacles to give her this new heart. They had to believe that God had spared Megan's life for a purpose.

Wayne had no idea how many times he had gone to the blog followers for prayer, but he knew they would pray, so he would ask again:

• 3:00 p.m. Megan is in her room; surgery went well. A blood clot was at the base of the aorta and they believe they removed it all, but there is a small chance that a piece broke off. Please pray that God has and will protect her from any complications.

* * * * *

Since Megan was in the chemically induced sleep, the family didn't have much to do regarding

188

her care. They spent the afternoon visiting and responding to Facebook posts.

That evening Kathie celebrated her birthday with her parents, most of Wayne's family, and many friends in the 56ICU waiting room.

Kathie opened her cards and gifts much like Wayne had done just five days ago; however, the party spirit on this night was much more jubilant. Even though they still weighed the news of the stroke possibility, they knew they were celebrating much more than Kathie's birthday. They were celebrating *life*...and it was up to God to decide the quality of life for Megan.

* * * * *

Sharon was relieved when her daughter, Karen, arrived safely with Garrett and Logan. As Sharon embraced them, she thanked God for accepting her surrender but sparing her daughter.

In the waiting room, everyone told Karen what had happened within the last two days. Sharon's grandson Garrett summarized it best when he responded, "Our big God is a hero."

* * * * *

It was quite late, and most of the friends and family were gone when Wayne got a call from Channel 5. Viewers were calling the station wanting an update on Megan. The reporter asked, "Would you be willing to do an interview at six tomorrow morning?"

Wayne wasn't as eager to consent to this request. Six o'clock was early, and he was exhausted from his short nights and long, emotional days. Second, he had just received news

189

of Megan's possible stroke. How could he say she was doing great with this possibility looming over her? If he didn't say she was great, what would he say?

After a brief personal debate, he agreed that God was opening the door yet again to take Megan's miracle to the nations. Wayne reluctantly agreed. He would have to trust God to help him rest well tonight and then trust Him to give him the words to speak in the morning.

Chapter 21

Surrendering the Outcome

Monday, April 19

* * * * *

The air was brisk and the sun was still below
the horizon when Wayne walked to the plaza
across from Barnes at 5:50 a.m. The Channel 5
KSDK crew gave Wayne a few last minute
instructions and the taping started.

"Megan made it through the surgery
successfully and is currently in a chemically
induced sleep which will continue for another day
or two," Wayne said. He didn't mention the word
stroke, but he let the viewers know there could be
complications. He credited God for Megan's gift of

life and asked the viewers for their continued prayers.

After the interview, both the interviewer and the cameraman revealed that they were believers and that their churches had prayed for Megan since Kay Quinn's interview with Megan. Wayne thanked the men and thought, *Only heaven will reveal how many churches and people have prayed for Megan during these last few weeks!*

* * * * *

When Dr. Wang made his rounds that morning, he gave Wayne a good report. Megan was receiving a lot of steroid medication to ward off any rejection, which was causing some swelling, but everything was well within the realm of normal following a transplant.

"In fact," he said, "Megan's stats are perfect."

Wayne thanked Dr. Wang profusely for the skilled treatment that he had given Meg.

Shortly after Dr. Wang left the room, Kathie arrived and the nurse announced that she would lessen Megan's sedation just enough to see if Megan could respond to verbal prompts to move her hands and her feet.

"Megan will still appear asleep, but she should be able to hear you and follow your commands," the nurse explained.

This brief test would not totally eliminate the possibility that there had been a stroke, but it would lessen the concerns.

Wayne said loudly and methodically, "Megan, this is Dad. If you can hear me, squeeze my hand."

No response.

Kathie tried, "Megs, we love you! Squeeze our hands."

After only a few tries, Megan responded to the commands and was able to squeeze each hand. "Yeah, Meg, you did it!"

Megan moved both sides of her body, showing that both sides of her brain worked. The nurse explained that now they were going for the big test.

"Megan needs to get brain waves all the way to her extremities and show us she can move her feet." Mom and Aunt Sharon rubbed Megan's feet while Dad said, "Move your foot, Meg. Show me you can do it. Come on, girl; kick that foot."

For almost an hour, they repeated the commands with no response.

"She just doesn't want to wake up," the nurse said. "She was given a lot of steroids, and that makes it more difficult. Just keep trying."

So they did.

Why isn't she responding? Did she have a stroke? Will she ever walk again? Will she be able to talk when she wakes?

Still they repeated commands and prayed with all their hearts.

When the nurse was almost ready to give up, Megan started kicking both feet and moving both hands so furiously that she looked as if she were going to kick herself out of bed. Kathie and Sharon squealed as they held Megan down. The nurse hurried to the machine regulating the sedation, and with a click of a button, Megan returned to her restful, chemically induced sleep.

"Wow, she really showed off for us," the relieved nurse said.

"Thank you, Lord!" the three said in unison. They knew they had witnessed another answer to prayer.

Throughout the day the doctors and support staff gave glowing reports of Megan's acceptance of the donor heart and the response of her other organs to the new part of the body. In fact, her organs appeared elated to have a full pumping heart. Wayne needed to share the news of the good day with the world:

• 5:20 p.m. Equipment and IV bags have been disappearing from Megan's room. Docs are amazed at how well she is doing. The plan is to wake her in the morning and let her breathe on her own. God has been faithful and has honored the prayers of His people. May we all continue to give Him the praise as Megan travels her road of recovery.

All eyes in the waiting room were on Channel 4, KMOV-TV that evening to see the spot, "Woman recovering from 'miracle' heart transplant." The anchor said, "The prayers of a Ferguson family were answered early Sunday morning when their 23-year-old daughter received a heart transplant." Not only did the television station give God credit for Megan's miraculous receipt of a heart and recovery, but the *Online Globe Democrat,* once St. Louis's largest print newspaper, posted an article telling Megan's story, titled: "An Eleventh Hour Miracle." This was amazing that even the secular world was calling the events of the last few days a *true miracle* from God.

* * * *

Tuesday, April 20

Megan's night nurse gave Wayne and Kathie a glowing report on Tuesday morning.

"All of Megan's stats are perfect," he said. He told them that the day nurse would try to awaken Megan that morning. Kathie sent a text to Mandi, and she responded, "Will be there!"

Wayne was glad that the time of wondering about the stroke possibility would soon be over. He asked the blog followers to pray:

• 8:30 a.m. From the mouth of the overnight nurse, David, "It is remarkable that a patient who has had two assist devices and a transplant in two weeks is doing this well! Remarkable!" I said, "It's God," and the nurse agreed. They are beginning to wake her now so pray the extubation goes well and Megan wakes feeling like a new woman.

* * * * *

As the awakening process began, Mandi, Wayne, Kathie, and Sharon stood around Megan's bed rubbing her arms and legs and calling her name, but the constant commands and touch produced no response. The nurses even pulled Megan's eyelids open, but Megan slept.

Throughout the day, all attempts to wake Megan failed. At about 3:00 p.m., Wayne desperately needed a break, and Sharon joined her brother on a walk to Children's Hospital, which was connected to Barnes. Wayne hoped to talk with Duane, a gentleman whose children had attended the school where Wayne was principal and who worked at Children's Hospital.

195

Sharon knew Duane, too, and had gained a high respect for him when her grandson Garrett was seriously ill in Children's Hospital four years earlier. Duane had discovered that Garrett's daddy was in Iraq, so he went beyond the call of duty to assist Sharon and Karen.

At the reception desk, Wayne asked for his friend. In minutes, Duane greeted them with a hug and handshake. He already knew about Megan, so he asked questions and listened as Wayne talked about the miracles and the looming concern.

Just as Wayne finished his conversation with Duane, another former NCCS parent and her daughter entered the hospital.

"Oh, Mr. Moss, it is so good to see you," they cried. "We saw Megan's interview on TV and have been praying for her. Our church has been praying, too."

Wayne and Sharon left Children's Hospital renewed and reminded of how widespread the rippling effect of this miracle was becoming.

It was nearing four o'clock when they returned to Megan's room. Kathie reported that she and Mandi had been unsuccessful; Meg still had not responded to any verbal commands. Since the daytime doctors would be leaving soon, the medical team decided to stop the awakening attempts for the day.

The attending physician in charge of anesthesiology assured the family that Megan's extreme sleepiness could have been due to her small size and the amounts of steroids she was given. Because Megan needed nutrition, they inserted a feeding tube into her nose. Before leaving for the evening, the doctor said, "There is never a smooth road to recovery, and everyone's bumps are at different spots."

* * * * *

One of Megan's Christian friends from the Ritz sent an email and noted that an unbelieving friend had approached him at work that day and said, "With all this that has happened to Megan, it's hard not to believe in God."

This was another vivid reminder that God's perspective and mission were much greater than Megan's hospital room.

All evening, reports flowed in of people who had come to faith over the weekend through Megan's miracle. The family continued to rebuke the Spirit of Fear and embrace the Spirit of Praise. God's Name would receive glory through their responses to whatever God chose to do.

* * * * *

Wednesday, April 21

Since Megan's transplant, everyone who entered her room wore masks and was sanitized to keep Megan and her room germ-free. During the night, however, Kathie's sniffles turned into a full-blown cold. Wanting to be near Megan, she got a prescription, wore a mask at all times, and took every precaution. Meanwhile, the family prayed for Kathie's recovery and for Megan's protection from the virus.

While they waited for the awakening process, Sharon asked Wayne about their financial need.

197

Wayne told her the bills had already exhausted Megan's savings. He smiled and said, "So it looks like she'll probably live at home a while longer, but that's okay with me."

Wayne then shared how God had been providing. Friends, family, and his church had given donations. NCCS was planning a benefit barbecue, and Bret Freeman was organizing a golf tournament benefit on Megan's birthday in May. Kyle and Mandi had also sold "I Love Meg" t-shirts to help with expenses. He grinned and said, "And two little girls gave me $30.88 that they earned at their lemonade stand for Megan last week. God will provide."

At 8:30 a.m. the nurse began lessening the sedation and encouraged the family to resume their verbal commands and touch. While they spoke to her and rubbed her limbs, they asked God to give her an easy, pleasant awakening.

The doctors had warned that the post-transplant medications could cause Megan to be delirious and agitated when she woke, but this time Megan woke easily. The respirator was removed, she breathed well on her own, and her sweet, even smile and soft words confirmed that there was no sign of a stroke.

Wayne felt as if the weight of the world had been lifted from his shoulders. That evening his rejoicing heart led him to the blog to give God praise:

• 5:30 p.m. We are praising God for Megan's improvement throughout the day. Doctors and nurses are shocked, but we know the source of her improvement. God is still performing His miracle on Megan. *Thank you, Jesus, for allowing all of us to be part of a modern-day miracle.*

Only an hour and a half later, Megan began experiencing a lot of pain. Wayne's belief in the power of prayer took him again to the blog followers:

• 7:10 p.m. Although Megan looks beautiful, she is in a lot of pain. Please pray that she will get relief soon so she can get good rest tonight. Don't mean to bother you with more requests, but every time you go to prayer, God answers.

Wayne realized how much he had come to depend on the prayers of the blog followers, most of them total strangers. These followers had become a powerful, unseen strength that God had provided for this time.

Wayne didn't realize that his belief in the prayers of his blog followers was actually increasing their faith. People who weren't sure they'd ever seen God specifically answer their prayers before began checking the blog so they'd know how to pray for Megan. They prayed for the specific needs, and then read in the next blog how God had answered. With each request, they prayed with more faith. With each answer, they praised God more fervently.

Chapter 22

Bumps in the Road

Thursday, April 22

* * * * *

A midnight x-ray was taken to determine the source of Megan's persistent chest pain. The x-ray revealed excessive air in her chest cavity around the left lung. Although the resident doctor was ready to do a procedure to release the air, another doctor insisted on an additional x-ray. The x-ray showed improvement, and each x-ray taken throughout the early morning hours was better. By sunrise Megan's pain was under control, and the doctors hoped the air would dissipate without a chest tube.

At noon another x-ray was taken, and the family hoped for a perfect report. Some air remained, but the doctors were willing to wait, and the blog followers were still willing to pray.

Megan continued to feel better. Her many nurse-assisted leg exercises were punctuated by breathing treatments: three deep breaths every ten minutes with the Airlife tube. Then it was time for physical therapy, and Megan would stand for the first time in twenty-two days.

With support from a nurse on each side, Megan sustained an upright position for several seconds. The joy of her accomplishment, however, was overshadowed by the overwhelming realization of her physical weakness.

Standing is so natural. How could it be so difficult? Megan thought.

Megan lowered herself into the recliner. She sat contemplatively in its safety for two and a half hours.

Kathie and Wayne spent much of the afternoon reading the email cards that continued to pour in from friends and strangers around the world. Megan occasionally responded with a few words as she watched her mom and dad laugh, cry, and praise the Lord over other miracles that were happening because people had faith for Megan's heart.

Even after Megan was back in bed for the evening, she didn't nap much. Kathie was concerned. "You seem a little sad, and you've hardly slept. What's going on, Megs?"

Megan admitted that she was very tired but explained, "Every time I think of going to sleep, I remember the awful nightmares I had after the

LVAD surgery. I'm afraid that when I close my eyes, those horrible faces will come back."

Kathie rubbed her precious daughter's hand and reminded her, "Speak the name of Jesus and the powers of darkness have to flee."

After praying with Meg, she tucked the blankets around her face, dimmed the light, and kissed her forehead.

* * * * *

Friday, April 23

Megan had a restful, nightmare-free sleep. That was good because she had a busy day ahead: breathing treatments, multiple physical therapy sessions, more x-rays, and the change of an IV port to ward off the possibility of infection.

Since she'd stood well the previous day, the therapist challenged her to try three forty-second periods of standing. Megan hoped she was ready for the challenges.

A doctor entered and exclaimed, "Megan, you are a miracle!"

Although he had not met Megan, his medical report file showed him evidence of many miracles in these last several days. The fact that Megan Moss was alive proved to him that the hand of the Great Physician was more powerful than medical science.

Trying to remember that she was a miracle, Megan did her best to meet each challenge. But after each successful try at standing, she sat in her chair and thought about all the things she used to do in a normal day. Megan had expected to wake from her transplant with renewed strength, ready to return to her busy world. Instead, she discovered she couldn't even stand by herself.

She contemplated the long road of recovery ahead and prayed that God would give her patience, and added, "And if you don't mind, God, please speed up the process. I really want to get better—fast!"

Until that prayer was answered, however, Megan knew she would have to accept help like a baby learning developmental skills for the first time.

Megan's swollen left leg was heavy and difficult to move; it didn't even look like it belonged with the rest of her thin body. By mid-afternoon a Doppler study was ordered to rule out the possibility of a blood clot.

Wayne asked the blog followers to help him pray:

• 3:00 p.m. The results of the Doppler study confirmed a blood clot. The doctor said, "Although the blood clot is a concern, it is not uncommon. I don't feel it will cause any problems." He assured the family that the weekend staff would watch Megan closely and do more tests on Monday.

Wayne asked for prayer again:

• 4:20 p.m. The heart rate has dropped, but there is a blood clot behind her knee. They are giving meds to try to dissolve it. Pray that it won't move and that it will be dissolved quickly. God is continuing His miracle.

* * * * *

The family had a secret that was keeping their hearts happy despite the blood clot. A Heartfelt

Celebration would take place on Saturday at 1:00 p.m. at the edge of Forest Park by Kingshighway Boulevard in view of Megan's fifth-floor windows. Everyone was told to wear red or their "I Love Meg" t-shirts and stand in the shape of a big heart to publicly praise God for His great miracle and brighten Megan's day.

Megan went to sleep early. She had experienced only minimal pain, and her spirits were slightly better; but she was still weak and exhausted.

* * * * *

Saturday, April 24

Megan enjoyed another restful night of dreamless sleep and woke eager to eat. However, it took her two hours to consume apple juice, a muffin, and vanilla pudding.

Megan reminded her dad that she had a valid excuse; she had to stop every 10 minutes to do the "three deep inhales" on the Airlife tube. And besides, she didn't want to eat too fast and have her food reappear. Thankfully her slow breakfast stayed put.

While Megan rested, Kathie cornered a nurse and explained the plans for the Heartfelt Celebration. She asked, "Would you help us find a way to get Megan to the window at one o'clock?"

The nurse said she would build the walk to the window into Megan's physical therapy.

Although Megan wasn't as sleepy and appeared stronger, she looked sad. Kathie questioned Meg, but she always responded, "I'm okay." Aware that patients often fight medicine-related depression after a transplant, Kathie prayed that God would bring the sparkle back into Meg's eyes.

Shortly after lunch the nurse announced, "Megan, you need to sit in the recliner for a while. After you've rested from the move, we'll help you walk just a few steps."

The nurse moved the recliner to the opposite side of the bed. Once the recliner was in place, with some assistance, Megan transferred to it and was pleasantly surprised by her increased strength.

Megan's chair faced away from the windows so she didn't notice her aunt, mom, and dad peering out the window, watching the celebration preparations. They could even identify many faces and watched as Kyle and a few other men put up a small tent while Mandi and others set up the table to sell "I Love Meg" t-shirts.

As the participants gathered, the rain clouds were gathering, too, and looked ominous. But those below were determined to celebrate rain or shine. Many asked God to stall the rain until after the celebration. By 1:00 p.m. the nurse received the go-ahead from Kathie and said, "Megan, we'll help you stand and turn around. Then we'll support you while you take a few steps toward the window."

Even though Aunt Sharon and Dad stood by the window and Mom was positioned with her camera, Megan didn't suspect anything. She assumed everyone was excited and ready to document her first steps.

Megan was up, her gown was adjusted, and her tubes were situated so she could turn. She was ready. Step one, step two, and step three. Megan looked into Forest Park and saw sixty friends and family members standing in the shape of a heart—waving and shouting.

Megan's mouth fell open.

Then she smiled.

Megan waved and the people in the heart went crazy. Traffic on Kingshighway, which ran between the park and the hospital, slowed as drivers looked at the shouting people and the waving patient at the window.

Someone shouted, "Let's all huddle, jump, and shout."

From Megan's fifth-floor room, the jumping looked like a beating heart. Yes, Megan had a healthy, beating heart and a happy smile.

The group at the window could tell everyone was singing and shouting. Though they couldn't hear what was being said, they knew God was being glorified and Megan was being loved.

Kathie expressed her desire to write "Thanks" on the window, and a nurse ran from the room. She returned with a roll of white surgical tape, tore off pieces, and handed them to Kathie. When the crowd below saw the white block letters that read, "Thanks!" they cheered again. Megan's nurses didn't remember ever having this much positive excitement in 56ICU.

When the celebration was almost over, two fire trucks arrived and parked in front of the group. Wayne called Shar and asked, "What's going on? Are the firefighters asking you to leave?"

Shar replied, "Oh, no! It's just Dale Schultz, and he brought a t-shirt for Megan."

Dale was a good friend who had grown up in Wayne's church. Wayne laughed and told Shar, "Well, tell Dale to get on that ladder and come on up and show the shirt to Megan."

As a few raindrops began to fall, Dale jumped on the ladder truck. Megan and the others watched in amazement as Dale rode the ladder up, up, up, until he was in front of Megan's fifth-story window. As he opened up the hot pink t-shirt to show her the black "St. Louis Fire Dept." words, he mouthed, "We're praying for you!"

The participants and Megan were grateful for Dale's grand finale to the celebration. As Megan was helped back to her chair, the rain began to pour. The participants ran for their vehicles and headed home.

Megan's oxygen level improved so much that afternoon that the nurse decided to remove the cannula from Megan's nose to see how she would do without oxygen support. Megan's lungs were strong, and her oxygen level remained stable. The medical team decided that it was time to remove another bothersome tube and machine.

When Megan's dinner tray came, she was strong enough to feed herself. By that evening, she was doing so well that the resident doctor decided to move her to the step-down unit. Although this unit was prepared to handle heart and lung emergencies, it did not have the same personnel ratio as ICU.

Wayne felt anxious about the move. He was concerned that Megan had a blood clot, was on a blood thinner, and the procedure to remove the neck port had been postponed until the next day.

Wayne and Sharon approached the resident doctor persistently asking that Megan stay in ICU until after the procedure in the morning. The request to remain in ICU was finally granted.

The local news that night showed the Heartfelt Celebration participants and Megan waving from the fifth-floor window. It also featured a clip of Dale on the ladder truck holding the t-shirt for Megan to see. The anchor said, "The St. Louis Fire Department went to great lengths today to bring a smile to the face of recovering Megan Moss."

Dale became known as the hero with a big heart.

* * * * *

Sharon sensed that it was time to go home. Megan was past the critical period, and Wayne and Kathie could now make it fine without her.

If all went well with the procedure in the morning, this would be Sharon's last night to sleep on the tiny love-seat in Consult Room #2.

God hadn't answered Sharon's prayer that Megan would have a bumpless recovery. Instead He allowed several bumps, which continued to build faith in His children. Now the family and friends surrounding Megan could see that the recovery was just as much a miracle as the transplant. Would they learn to trust God with all of the bumps in the roads of their lives?

Chapter 23

Learning Patience

Sunday, April 25

* * * * *

Sharon was up early so she could be the first to shower and then pack for home. When she arrived in Megan's room, Wayne told her the procedure to remove the neck port hadn't been done yet and that Kathie had already left to clean up at the Ritz. Wayne's Bible was open to Lamentations 3 on the special words of encouragement God had given to Kathie so many weeks earlier.

Before Wayne finished reading the scripture passage, Dr. Wang arrived, home from the conference he had attended since Tuesday. Dr. Wang announced that after reviewing Megan's records, he had decided to take her off the Heparin for at least four hours before the neck port procedure. This would give Megan's blood time to thicken and would lessen the bleeding risk.

* * * * *

Megan was celebrating her one-week heart birthday, and today she would make her epic journey down the hall. The nurse informed Megan that they would attempt only a short distance, but if she felt up to walking farther she could.

Since Megan's sparkle had returned on Saturday, she was eager to jump each hurdle in the recovery process and return to normal. The nurse showed up with her assistant who carried a portable oxygen tank and explained that patients often need a little oxygen on their first walk. Wayne would push a chair behind Megan in case she needed to rest.

As Megan walked into the hallway, she thought of all her cross-country runs; she could do this. She walked past a few rooms and decided she could handle a few more. Her legs were wobbly but stronger than they had been, so she counted off a few more rooms. The nurses praised her and insisted that she rest. Megan complied but wanted to keep walking.

Several times Dad and the nurses encouraged Megan to turn around, but she was determined to complete the task. When she approached her room after completing the circle past all 25 rooms in the unit, the nurse said, "Megan, most patients on their first walk can only pass a few rooms. You walked approximately 360 feet which is farther than the length of a football field." The nurse told Megan the medical staff was amazed by her progress.

* * * * *

When Sharon, Karen, and her boys finished their lunch and returned to the waiting room,

Wayne and Kathie were talking with Jason and Dani. The medical team had just begun the procedure to remove the neck port.

In anticipation of a good report from Megan's procedure, Sharon emptied her locker and carried all her bags and bedding to her car.

The procedure went smoothly, and Sharon sensed that the family had begun a new chapter in Megan's miracle story. Sharon gave her family one last hug and headed home.

* * * * *

Megan was to stay in 56ICU one more night. Wayne and Kathie were thankful that Meg would have another day of constant supervision from the awesome staff that had become like family to them. It would also give Megan one more day to get stronger before leaving the comfort of familiarity.

Before sleeping in the recliner that night, Kathie sent a message to her Facebook friends at 11:33 p.m. "Returning from the Come to the Fire conference in early November, we discussed transferring our faith to the next generation. I pray that Megan's story will play a part in making that happen. *Let each generation tell its children of your mighty acts; let them proclaim your power* (Psalm 145:4). God still moves mightily today."

* * * * *

Monday, April 26

The nurse informed Megan that this would be a busy day so Kathie asked for specific prayer cover from their Facebook friends. Wayne then copied her post into his blog:

- 8:50 a.m. Megan is doing well this morning and is getting ready to start her daily activities: walk around the unit; heart biopsy (pray for NO rejection); echocardiogram (pray for a good ejection fraction), lunch (pray for her appetite to totally return), and move to step-down unit. Recovery is in fast-forward. Praise God!

Dr. Wang checked Megan's chest incision. He told her that he had shown the picture of her in the shuttle, the huge therapeutic chair, at the conference. Dr. Wang looked at Megan and then said, "I think you might want to know that when I was preparing your chest for the receipt of the new heart, I barely pressed against your LVAD incision, and was able to simply pull your chest open with my hands."

Kathie interjected, "Good. Then you didn't have to use the saw."

Dr. Wang responded, "That was not a good thing. Because Megan's chest came open that easily, it meant she was so sick her incision had not healed at all since her LVAD surgery two weeks earlier. If I had known she hadn't healed, I would not have been able to do the transplant."

But God wanted the surgery done, it was done, and Megan was doing well. This miracle deserved a big Ebenezer stone!

Megan was moved to the step-down unit after 26 days in ICU. The nurses even brought in a bed so Kathie wouldn't have to sleep in the recliner.

Since Meg was doing well and would be out of the room taking tests for most of the day, Kathie decided to go back to real life for a while. She returned home—to that place of comfort she'd seen very little of that month. She did laundry, paid bills, and played with her granddaughter, Kinsley.

She remembered, "This is what life felt like before November 30 and Megan's congestive heart failure."

She thanked God for His care during these months, but she longed to return to the normal days of family life at home.

* * * * *

Megan and her dad had a good day together between the therapies and tests. Although the biopsy rejection level results would not be available until Tuesday, Megan was told her heart pressure was three months ahead of schedule.

"Praise the Lord!" Wayne said. The medical team declared that this was remarkable. Wayne thought, *I think I've heard that word remarkable before. God has done a perfect work in Megan!*

Kathie returned to Barnes in time to see Megan eagerly eating her dinner. She praised God for Megan's appetite and His plan for nutritious food that heals and maintains health. Kathie also learned that Megan had walked around the unit twice with little assistance.

Since Megan was having some pain from the biopsy, she was relieved that the medical team had run out of time to do the echocardiogram. She just wanted to sleep. She was confident that her parents' Facebook friends and blog followers would pray while she slept and God would answer.

* * * * *

It was such a busy morning that Wayne didn't have time to update the blog followers until the afternoon.

• 1:20 p.m. Busy day. Meg walked 420 feet, doctor's visit, therapy, and lots of meeting new people on the new floor. She had lots of pain last night, but it's now under control. Still no word on the biopsy, but we'll assume no news is good news. Prayer request: her left chest tube is leaking fluids and her nutritional level is still low. They still are amazed at her progress.

Megan finally had her echocardiogram and then took a second walk around the unit: a whopping 700 feet. She was told she could go back to bed for a nap, but she felt so well, she said, "I'd rather sit in the chair, thank you."

Wayne knew his girl was getting better.

The doctor appeared with a smile that stretched the width of the Golden Gate Bridge. The heart biopsy showed the rejection factor to be 1A: essentially no rejection, an absolutely awesome reading.

The report from the echocardiogram was also back. A normal person's ejection fraction (EF) is between 50-75 percent. Megan's EF registered 55-60 percent. This was unheard of. God had done His perfect work.

Wayne and Kathie thanked God for the great reports and asked their friends to continue praying.

* * * * *

Several doctors continued to use the word *miracle* when they talked of Megan's transplant and recovery. In fact, one doctor said, "Megan, your recovery is the one to beat."

There were several answers to prayer that day. Megan's nutritional levels were better, and the feeding tube was removed. Megan also learned another chest tube would come out later in the day.

Along with the good news was another possible bump in the road. The doctor suspected the presence of another blood clot so ordered a Doppler study on Megan's legs. The technician doing the procedure told the family they would have the results within twenty-four hours.

Kay Quinn from Channel 5 requested another interview with Megan. The hospital video team also joined Kay as Megan showed the world what her God and the skilled hands of the Barnes' staff had done. When the media personnel left, Megan was ready for a long nap.

After the evening news, Wayne and Kathie discussed again how unbelievable it was that people continued to show interest in Megan's progress. It had to be God drawing people to watch Him at work in her.

They were discussing the far-reaching effect of Megan's journey when they received a Facebook post from one of Kathie's childhood friends:

"Kathie—I haven't seen you in years—but your daughter was amazing in the interview. Her sweetness, genuine appreciation, concern for others, and gratitude was so obviously real. I have a wonderful 21-year-old daughter—my best hope is that she would have the same grace and inner beauty in such trying times. Thanks for sharing this time with those of us following the blog and Facebook."

Megan did have an inner strength that came from God, but she was human and struggled with her limitations. Her lack of independence was emotionally difficult. She knew the step-down unit was to prepare her to care for herself at home, but she wondered if the nurses really understood her weakness—they expected her to do so much more than she seemed physically capable of doing.

On several occasions Megan pushed the nurse-call button when she needed the bedside commode in the night but waited for what seemed like an eternity. One night as she waited, she swung one leg off the bed but then realized she couldn't pull her body to a sitting position. She knew she wasn't supposed to strain her chest muscles, but she held the rail of the bed and tried to pull herself up. No amount of determination could make it happen.

I am totally helpless: I can't sit up, stand up, or even get on a toilet by myself, she thought. When the nurse arrived, Megan was more eager than ever to have the emotional roller coaster and the inconveniences of her physical weakness behind her.

As Megan tried to return to sleep, she not only rehearsed her inability to sit up, but she thought about the results of the Doppler test she would receive in the morning.

How much more can I take? she wondered. But with strength that came from within, she repeated her motto, "Through this I demonstrate that Christ is enough—come what may!" Then added, "And,

Jesus, no matter what the report says, please help me to be patient."

Chapter 24

Ready for Anything

Thursday, April 29

* * * * *

The Doppler study showed Megan had developed four small blood clots in her legs and one in her neck. The one in the neck was the greatest concern because it was close to the heart, but the doctor said, "All of the clots are small and treatable."

He did, however, reiterate one major problem: the blood clots needed to clear quickly because the Heparin would increase the risk of bleeding during the necessary weekly biopsies.

Wayne responded, "Doctor, do what you need to do to treat the blood clots. We'll pray that the clots will dissolve and that God will give you wisdom for Megan's care."

It was a busy day once Megan's exit plan was put in place. It would be several days before Megan's release, but the routine tests needed to be scheduled and the home-care treatment plan had to be taught to the caregivers. Megan, Kathie, and Wayne didn't realize how much they had to learn and do, preparing for a transplant patient going home.

As the day progressed, Kathie realized the family needed additional prayers. At 9:14 p.m. she wrote on Facebook: "Today we met a man who had his heart transplant 14 years ago. We met a sweet mom whose four-month-old daughter received her new heart this week. Loving friends brought dinner again tonight! We have so many people to thank for walking this journey with us. You know who you are...friends we know and friends we just haven't met yet. Today, it seemed that every department in this hospital had something to teach us before Meg goes home. Here are some specifics to help you pray for Megan:

"Blood clots—four or five small ones are being treated. Not a huge worry, we're told, but they will watch this.

"Swelling—lots. This is normal after surgery and because of the clots. But it's uncomfortable and *heavy*. I'm not sure we have to settle for normal. I think God just might be able to take care of this, too!

"Lungs—pleural effusion. There's extra air in the pocket around the lung that needs to dissipate. If it gets worse, a tiny chest tube will be inserted to remove the air.

"Strength—increasing every day. She has lost all muscle tone, and one med increases big muscle wobbliness.

"Emotions—while meds are being adjusted, Meg can have emotional highs and lows. This will probably be one of the most difficult things for Meg to deal with! Hebrews 11:1 is shining through with all its glory. It was the certainty to know that what we hoped for was waiting for us ahead—we just couldn't see it—but He did."

* * * * *

Friday, April 30

At 8:00 a.m. Kathie sat by sleeping Meg and read old Facebook posts. She felt the urge to create a recap for her friends, a reminder of things God had done. She wrote: "Sitting here with Megan watching her sleep so peacefully and reading old FB posts: 'Meg is on life support...struggling for every breath...Meg woke during procedure and bleeding...we have a heart...the heart is beating...Sleeping Beauty woke today...' *God, I am so thankful for all You've done and are going to do in our lives as we continue to trust You each day for continued healing for Megan.*"

When Megan woke from her nap, she took a few laps around the unit. On one lap, she said, "One of the most difficult things for me after the transplant was realizing I couldn't walk."

Megan told her mom how she was learning to appreciate every part of her wonderful body that God had created. She would never again take for granted the ability to breathe, sit up, or walk on her own.

"And, what a blessing it will be," she emphasized, "to be able to walk free of tubes and machines."

Megan anticipated the removal of another tube that day. Then she would have only the heart monitor and one more IV bag and she would be a free woman.

Another thing that Megan determined never to under-appreciate was the power of prayer. The night before, Megan had gone to sleep with so many extra pounds of fluid in her body that she ached everywhere. Mom sent a prayer call for her swelling, and Megan saw the signs of answered prayer throughout the day as her legs became thinner and thinner.

"Mom, I don't ever want to forget that I *saw* a miracle today!" she exclaimed.

* * * * *

Saturday, May 1

Finally the unforgettable April had ended. The Mosses were embarking on a new month and a new life for Megan. The family recalled the eventful Saturday four weeks earlier when Megan was put on the LVAD and then the traumatic Saturday just two weeks earlier when Megan hovered between life and death. But, thanks to God and His mercy, this would be a Saturday of rejoicing with Megan's first *real* bath in a month.

The nurses let Megan disconnect the heart monitor and IV bag so she could experience a few moments of freedom. Megan didn't have enough strength to stand, so she sat on a shower chair. The uncontrollable shivering exhausted her strength, and realizing her mom had to do almost everything for her drained her emotional reserves.

The monitor and IV were reattached, and it was time for another x-ray to check the air around her lungs. Megan was praying that it had decreased. She wanted to be done with body punctures and miscellaneous tubes.

Before Wayne slept that night he wrote:

• 9:40 p.m. X-rays were better, so no tube is needed. Kathie, Meg, and I took a 20-minute walk tonight up and down her hall. We would have liked to show Meg more of the hospital, but her heart monitor would have set off an alarm at the nurses' station.

* * * * *

Sunday, May 2

Wayne wondered if Saturdays and Sundays would ever be *just normal* again, or would he always relive the eventful Saturday and Sunday that gave new life to his Meg.

Megan had worn the drab hospital gowns long enough. With fewer bags and tubes to worry about, she put on her Sunday best: the brightly colored hospital gown her Aunt Shar had purchased for her. Wayne couldn't resist a picture; he showed the blog followers that his girl was looking great.

Wayne's late evening blog read:

• 8:40 p.m. Megan had a great day! She has walked over 3,000 feet today. Tomorrow is the heart biopsy; pray that there will be no rejection. If that is the case, the plan is to be home Tuesday!

Just minutes later, Megan walked unassisted. This happy dad took another picture and made another post. Wayne wanted God to receive the glory for every part of this miracle journey, and this was an important step: Meg was stable and getting stronger.

* * * * *

Monday, May 3

Anticipating Megan's homecoming, some of Kathie's friends planned a cleaning and lawn mowing party. As friends dusted, vacuumed, shined the bathrooms, and mowed the lawn, Megan and Kathie were learning about all the medication rituals they'd follow when they got home. Megan was then taken for her weekly biopsy.

When Wayne and Kathie noticed fluid oozing from Megan's tube sites, they wondered if this would keep Megan from going home. The nurse explained that it was just fluid that had built up since the surgery.

"But how could fluid oozing from wounds be normal?" they asked. Nevertheless, they chose to continue to trust in the prayers of their friends, in the providence of God, and in the medical staff. Megan would go home when God was ready for her to go home.

* * * * *

Tuesday, May 4

It had been over five months since the congestive heart failure diagnosis and a long thirty-five days since the admission to the Cardiac ICU. But only 18 days had passed since the no-hope day when God's people stormed heaven and God gave a miracle.

Megan's reports on this day were incredible. The biopsy report came back with "0" percent rejection, and the echocardiogram produced an EF of 65 percent. These were not the numbers of a heart transplant patient; these were the numbers of a perfect-match heart given by the Great I Am.

"We have one last x-ray to take, and you'll be headed home," the doctor announced.

Well, so much for one last x-ray. The x-ray went fine, but 101 other things needed to be done before Megan could leave. While Megan was getting dressed, her tube site began gushing fluid again. The fluid soiled Megan's clothes and soaked through several bandages. Kathie was sure that this development would keep Meg from going home. In fact, she wasn't sure she wanted to take her daughter home with fluid pouring from her.

The nurses simply bandaged the area again and again until the draining slowed. They smiled and handed Megan several boxes of bandages to take home.

After all the delays and excitement, at 6:00 p.m. Megan and her parents pulled into the driveway of their home. Friends had placed "Welcome Home" signs and balloons everywhere.

This was a time to celebrate, but emotions from April 1 flooded Megan's mind...that dark day when her daddy had to carry her to the car...the day she knew she would never see her home again unless God provided a donor heart. And here she was at home—with a second chance at life with a new heart.

Although the sun would be setting soon, this was a day of new beginnings.

Chapter 25

When Life and Death Don't Make Sense

Wednesday, May 5 through Thursday, May 11

* * * * *

With the arrival of daylight on May 5, Megan realized that it wasn't a dream; she was at home in her own comfy bed. And she wasn't attached to any tubes or wires. She thought about the many things she'd like to do on her first day home, but when she tried to get out of bed, she realized she was still quite weak. She decided to focus on the things she *could* do rather than all the things she couldn't do *yet*. Megan was sure it would be a good day because she was home.

Kathie was also glad to be at home. She had a long list of things to do and began by unpacking and doing laundry. Kathie's most important job today, though, was to create some nutritious food so her 87-pound Megs would gain some weight.

By the time Megan and Kathie ate their breakfast, Wayne was back at school and fully acclimated to the energy that children bring with them to the classroom. In his office, he realized how much catch-up work he had. The duties before him were overwhelming, but with God's help, he could do it.

Often throughout the day, Megan, Kathie, and Wayne felt grateful for the mundane things of life.

* * * * *

The next day was a warm, beautiful Thursday with spring in the air. Kathie thought of the many miracles and blessings of the last five weeks. She told her Facebook friends, "Sometimes I feel afraid that as we get back to normal life, I will forget the many incredible things that God did to get us to this point. I pray that that will never happen. I want to always be aware of the miracle of Megan's life."

Friday was another blessed day of routine. Wayne, Kathie, and Megan enjoyed a relaxing evening at home with a movie and popcorn, small pleasures they'd previously taken for granted.

Saturday was a perfect day for the benefit barbeque at North County Christian School. Kathie stayed with Meg while Wayne went to thank Megan's supporters and encourage the participants to be organ donors. Wayne was so grateful to be a part of God's family as he later told Kathie about all of the people who planned, cooked, performed, donated, and attended the fundraiser. He was overwhelmed by the many people who gave love and support though they didn't even know Megan.

* * * * *

On Mother's Day, Sunday, May 9, Kathie's first thoughts were of the mother of the 30-year-old female donor. She prayed that God would hold that mom in His loving arms on this first Mother's Day without her daughter.

Wayne offered to stay home with Meg so Kathie could go to church, but she wanted to stay home with her girl. Megan had missed celebrating Easter with the family, so she had insisted on a big Mother's Day dinner with Grandma and Grandpa Moss and the other St. Louis family members. Megan helped plan the menu, and everyone would bring one of her favorite foods. As Kathie prepared a casserole, she was surprised to hear Megan calling for her.

* * * * *

Near the beginning of the worship service, Kathie texted Wayne: "Meg woke with chest pain."

He responded, "Call the doctor."

Near the end of the service, Wayne received another text: "Need to take Meg to ER." Before the benediction, Wayne interrupted the pastor and asked if they could pray for Meg. While the congregation prayed, Wayne hurried home.

Meg had begun throwing up and her pain was increasing to the point that she could barely lift her left arm or sit up.

As Kathie put the Mother's Day meal back in the refrigerator, she said, "Well, we celebrated

Easter at Barnes, and I guess we'll have our Mother's Day celebration there, too."

While Kathie and Megan got ready, Wayne called the blog followers to prayer. On the way to the hospital Kathie texted family members. This sure wasn't the Mother's Day that any of the family wanted.

* * * * *

Sharon had just arrived home from church when Shar called to tell her Megan was in the ER.

"We have to believe that this is just another part of our miracle," Shar added.

Sharon tried to believe that her sister's words were true, but she leaned over her kitchen counter and wept. She had spent the previous day typing the journal she'd kept in the hospital so Kathie could have a list of all the miracles and blessings during the April hospital stay. Kathie was supposed to spend the next week documenting miracles on stones, not caring for Megan in the hospital again.

"Oh, God, You and Meg took me on an incredible faith journey that I will never forget or question," Sharon prayed. "So help me not to harbor fear now. Instead, may this bump in the road keep me on my knees in anticipation of another miracle."

* * * * *

The emergency room doctor admitted Megan and sent her for tests. Kathie stayed with Megan while Wayne took their belongings to Megan's room. As he unloaded his arms, he received a text.

"Jimmy and Josh Farrar were in an accident. Jimmy died and Josh is in serious condition."

This can't be happening, Wayne thought. Jimmy was like a son to Wayne. He had watched him grow up at NCCS, and when Jimmy's parents moved to Troy, a 45-minute drive from Ferguson, Jimmy still wanted to attend and graduate from NCCS. When there were late night ballgames, Jimmy often stayed overnight at Wayne's house. Since Megan and Jimmy were in the same class, he had become like a brother to Megan. Wayne wiped tears and thought, *How can I possibly tell Meg?*

* * * * *

Before long Megan settled in her room and the pain medication had her smiling again. While she rested, Wayne pulled Kathie to the hall and told her about the Farrar boys. They asked the medical personnel what they should do about telling Megan.

"Oh, please don't tell her yet; it would be too hard on her heart," the team responded.

Wayne felt that he had to check on Josh and comfort this family. As soon as he was sure Megan was stable, he kissed his wife and daughter good-bye.

As Wayne drove the five miles to the hospital where doctors were frantically trying to save Josh, he tried to imagine what he could say. When he got there, Wayne simply cried with the family. He thought of the friends and family who had stayed with him during the dark hours in April and knew he couldn't leave this family tonight. He stayed and together they watched Josh pass from this world to the next.

Wayne needed his prayer warriors now more than ever. He couldn't share the Farrars' news, but his update on Meg would activate the prayers that he needed.

* * * * *

On Monday morning Megan and her family were relieved to learn that she only had some fluid build-up in the chest cavity, which was normal after a transplant. As the fluid drained naturally, Megan's pain medications would be adjusted to keep her comfortable. Megan could have gone home, but since she was due for her third weekly biopsy, her physician decided to keep her one more day. Megan got comfortable and asked for her laptop so she could connect with Facebook friends.

"Meg, before you open Facebook, I need to tell you something," Kathie said.

Kathie then told Meg that Jimmy and Josh had been killed in a car accident on Mother's Day. The day was difficult for Megan as she grieved this loss. She spent a lot of time on Facebook looking at the pictures of Jimmy and remembering his visit with her in the hospital a few weeks earlier.

All day Tuesday Megan waited for her biopsy, but it didn't happen. This meant she would have to spend another night at Barnes.

When Dr. Wang checked on her, he had a different opinion than the doctors who had examined Megan on Monday. He felt the fluid needed to be drained; there was just too much. He ordered a procedure for Wednesday morning.

Since so much of the ICU experience from the month before had been a blur for Megan, Wayne and Kathie took Meg on a walk that evening. They showed her Room #1 in 56ICU where she slept after the LVAD surgery and where the demons of darkness haunted her. But Megan focused on the chair where during her hallucinations she saw a man in white who came to protect her.

And then there was Room #12 with the gorgeous view of Forest Park where the Heartfelt Celebration took place. This was the room where she talked with Danny Gokey on the phone, did TV interviews, and enjoyed pleasurable conversations with her friends and family while being kept alive by the incredible LVAD. This was also the room where several bedside procedures had saved her life. This was the place where Megan hovered between life and death.

Room #12 was also the room where Dr. Ewald offered Megan a new heart. Megan said, "I will never forget his hug. It felt like when Jesus squeezed me during the procedure. Remember, the one when I was so scared and asked Mom to have the Facebook friends pray?"

This room also held the memories of her first days with a new heart: sitting, standing, and walking for the first time. There were memories of the bumps in the road but also the remarkable recovery and the bountiful blessings that God gave Megan and her family.

The walk down memory lane wouldn't have been complete without talking to some of their favorite nurses. Megan thanked them for the special care they'd given her, even when she was sleeping.

* * * * *

On Wednesday morning Megan asked the doctor, "Is there any way I can leave by noon? I want to attend my friend's funeral."

The doctor promised to release her as soon as possible. They decided not to do the biopsy because it would take too much time. Instead, they began the procedure to drain the fluid.

Megan had received so many incisions, pokes, and wounds in the last five months that sticking a needle and a small tube in her back didn't seem like much. As soon as the fluid was drained, the nurse put a bandage over the puncture wound and started the out-processing paperwork.

All of Megan's past dismissals had been late afternoon or evening, but this time Megan left the parking garage just past noon. Since Megan had lost so much weight, she knew she didn't have anything in her closet that fit. Megan had a plan: she would talk her mom into a quick shopping trip to her favorite store. She promised to wear a mask and let her mom touch doors and clothing racks for her.

Megan was slightly self-conscious shopping with a mask, but her self-esteem had gone through so many adjustments in the last few months that she realized her worth was in Christ, not in how people viewed her. On the ride home, she thought about how unbelievable it was that her first outing with her new heart was to buy an outfit for a friend's funeral.

* * * * *

As Megan listened to the memorial sermon, she thought of how this moment just didn't make sense.

Why did God spare my life but let these boys lose theirs? Why was my life spared, but a young adult woman died and her heart beats in my chest?

Megan could only conclude that life and death don't make sense except to God who knows His eternal plan for each individual.

After the service, Megan visited with high school friends. Although she had to refrain from touch since she was susceptible to germs, she sensed their love and concern. Megan realized that she no longer saw them as simply friends; they were eternal souls, and she wondered if they had dealt with their own mortality.

Do they realize that every breath is a gift from God? she wondered.

Megan walked from the memorial service realizing that she had been spared and given a second-chance at life for a reason—an eternal reason. She silently vowed, *God, I will find Your purposes for me and will live every day in grateful service for the blessing of life that You gave to me.*

Chapter 26

Accepting the Challenges

Friday, May 12 through Sunday, August 8

* * * * *

On Friday, May 12 Megan learned that her interview with the Barnes' newsroom several weeks ago had been turned into a front-page article in the hospital newspaper. She couldn't wait to see it the next time she was at the hospital.

Life was returning to normal for Megan but still offered daily challenges. On Saturday morning as Meg helped her mom clean up after breakfast, she looked longingly at the steep step into the laundry room and thought about all the steps she'd need to climb when she ventured into the outside world.

But this was only one step so she decided to try it. Going down was easy, but coming back up was more difficult than she expected. Megan was determined, though. She would practice several times a day until her muscle strength increased and responded when her brain told her legs to lift her body. She would conquer that step and then move to other challenges.

* * * * *

Megan's boss didn't want her to miss the annual gala where they honor their employees. After making sure that Megan was physically able to come, he arranged for a limo to pick up Megan and her parents on the evening of Sunday, May 16. When the luxurious ride to Clayton ended at the canopied door of the Ritz, Megan saw her boss, Andrew, waiting with a wheelchair. He greeted her with a hug, helped her out of the limo, and then wheeled her into the beautiful Ritz-Carlton Hotel. They enjoyed the gourmet meal in the privacy of a small quaint room where Megan was protected from public germs.

The program coordinator knew the employees wanted to see Megan, so he had given her the job of announcing the names of the top five employees of the year. This was an especially meaningful honor since Megan had received the award the year before.

After dinner it was time for Megan to stand behind the podium. A weak Megan clung to her dad as they approached the stage. When Wayne saw the steps Megan would have to climb to get to the platform, he told the program coordinator, "She can't walk up those steps; she's too weak."

While they contemplated how to get her to the platform, a manager insisted, "I'll carry her."

Wayne tried to protect his daughter's dignity, but Megan finally said, "Oh, just let him carry me."

As soon as he reached the top step, he let go and Megan's legs couldn't sustain her position and body weight. Wayne lunged to catch Meg as she slid to the floor.

Because of the gentle fall, Megan was emotionally and physically spent when she was handed the microphone. Her hand shook so intensely that Wayne held the mic for her and stood close to support her body.

As Megan descended the steps with her dad's support, she knew she had reentered the real world prematurely. She would have to limit her challenges.

The next morning, Megan rose early for a doctor's appointment. This would be one of many appointments during the next few months as she checked off the many milestones of recovery.

Today Dr. Wang would check her wound sites: the surgical incisions and the holes where tubes and ports had been inserted. This was important since infection was one of the greatest risks to recovery. Megan was relieved when everything checked out fine. This was another Ebenezer stone and a reason to praise God for His protection during the recovery process.

As Megan prepared to leave, Dr. Wang said, "Well, Megan, this is the last time you will have to see me, unless it's for social purposes."

Megan had developed a special relationship with this doctor. Dr. Wang had given her a beating heart, and she would forever be indebted to him for using his skill to give her life.

While Megan was at Barnes, a nurse handed her several copies of the hospital newspaper. Megan was surprised to see that her picture with Dr. Wang covered the front page, followed by a long article.

On the way home, Megan read the article to her mom. She began, "In the 25 years Barnes-Jewish has performed heart transplants, few have gained the celebrity of the 587th patient to receive a heart, 23-year-old Megan Moss. The attention Megan has received from the St. Louis community is anything but ordinary."

"Mom, listen to this!" Megan exclaimed. She continued reading, "To say it came down to the wire would be selling short what happened the day of April 17."

"Sounds like they are acknowledging a miracle," Kathie responded

Megan kept reading. "What followed was an unprecedented amount of emails for one patient through the Barnes-Jewish website."

Kathie knew that Meg had received a lot of email cards but was surprised to learn that during Megan's five weeks in the hospital she had received 432 email-cards—normally the amount the hospital gets in a month for all its patients.

The article asked readers to spread the need for organ donation since a growing list of people are on the heart transplant waiting list but only about 25 hearts are available every year. Megan continued, "Overall, the Moss family credits their faith for making this transplant possible. 'God has held us in his arms minute by minute, keeping us strong by His love and grace,' says Megan's mother

Kathie, who adds that a Bible verse has been very meaningful to her over the past few weeks. *Because of God's great love, I am not consumed. For His compassions never fail. They are new every morning; great is His faithfulness."*

"They even quoted your scripture," Megan said gratefully. "You go, God!"

On Thursday when Megan returned for another appointment, several people asked, "Are you the Megan who had the heart transplant?"

When she answered, "Yes," strangers encouraged her and many told how they had seen the television interviews, had followed her story on the blog, or had even prayed for her. Megan and her dad were again amazed by how God had truly gathered the multitudes to watch Him at work.

* * * * *

Saturday, May 22, was Megan's 24th birthday and the day of the golf benefit that would help Megan pay for her many medical bills. The event was a great success, and Kathie and Megan enjoyed riding in the decorated golf cart.

After the fundraiser, Megan's friends, Molly and Erin, dropped by the house to say, "Happy Birthday!" The three girls had always gone to dinner together since Molly shared Megan's birthday. But today would be different since Megan couldn't go to restaurants yet. After a visit, she watched her special friends drive away. She was eager for the day when they could go places together again.

The next day was another milestone in Megan's recovery: she joined her family for worship for the first time since early February. On that morning, praise was not only on their lips, it rose from their souls. God had been faithful through all these months.

* * * * *

Megan's diligence at conquering the laundry room step had paid off; she could soon climb the flight of steps from the basement. Daily she gained strength even though she wasn't gaining much weight.

"God is good; God is good all the time," became a phrase Megan repeated as she approached challenges and conquered them one by one.

At every appointment, the doctor lowered medicine dosages due to Megan's remarkable progress. The biopsies continued to confirm the complete acceptance of the donor heart. Wayne told his blog followers, "The doctors say *this is unheard of*, but I say *this is a miracle!*"

* * * * *

In June of 2010, Megan received permission to drive again. Although her mom still accompanied her to the many therapy visits and doctors' appointments, Megan could drive to the routine rehab walks in the mall. Her determination to conquer this challenge paid off. She weighed only 93 pounds when she began rehab but reached her goal of 100 pounds by the time she graduated from the program.

Also in June, Megan was strong enough to attend the annual Nazarene Camp Meeting with her family. The camp meeting was a week-long time of fellowship and spiritual renewal at a campground for those in the Nazarene denomination who lived within the same district as Megan's church. Megan accomplished another important goal during that week: she wore high heels. She was thrilled to dress up. The family told her, "You look good, girl!" And she did.

During camp Megan received an important phone call. The reports showed that all of the blood clots that had been in her neck were gone. These blood clots had been a real scare since they were so close to the brain, but God in His mercy had dissolved them.

"This miracle deserves an Ebenezer stone," Megan told the family.

The annual time of camp meeting had become not only an occasion for spiritual renewal, but for decades it had been a time for Wayne's extended family to visit, play games, and catch up on each others' lives. This year the focus was on Megan and the miracle.

Wednesday night after the camp meeting service, about twenty friends and family members gathered in Mom and Dad Moss' cabin to hear details of the prayer for Megan at MAX on the day when Meg was dying.

They learned that the prayer time was still having far-reaching effects on youth groups and churches in the seven-state region represented by MidAmerica Nazarene University.

During the camp meeting, the Mosses learned that many at camp had followed the blog, prayed, and were now rejoicing with the family as they watched God's miracle, Megan, walk across the grounds. Many people shared their stories of how God had used their prayers for Megan to change their own lives.

A few others didn't know the story so after the Thursday evening service, Wayne was asked to tell more than 100 people the *whole* story—well as much as Wayne could squeeze into an hour and a half. When Wayne finished, he was convinced God still wanted to use Megan's miracle to bring people to faith in Christ.

* * * * *

Wayne, Kathie, and Megan returned home after camp meeting for three days of normal life before returning to the same campgrounds for a family reunion for Mom Moss' side of the family. The three had some logistics to consider. Megan had a doctor's appointment on the second day of the reunion, but Wayne and Kathie really didn't want to miss any of the reunion.

Megan thought it was a no-brainer. Mom and Dad would go to the campgrounds whenever they wanted, and she would drive down after the appointment.

Wayne hesitated. It had been hard enough to let Megan resume driving around St. Louis, but a two-hour trip by herself was another matter. But Megan convinced her daddy.

At camp, Wayne told Sharon, "It feels weird being so anxious about my 24-year-old making this trip. I know she's an adult and a good driver, but it feels like I've handed the car keys to my toddler."

Within the span of ten weeks, Wayne had carried Meg, helped her stand for the first time, helped her relearn to walk, watched her relearn to climb steps, and now saw her driving. "At least I know she can call me if she needs me," he added.

Megan arrived safely and enjoyed the inspirational, fun family reunion with her relatives. Wayne summarized the time together:

• 7/4/10 Just got home from the MILLER 2010 REUNION. Reminded me once again of the awesome heritage we have because of the prayers of my grandparents, Art and Vera Miller. Megan, our most recent miracle, is just one of many miracles in this wonderful family. *Thank you, Grandma and Grandpa Miller, for praying for the future generations of the Miller family. Your prayers are answered each day.* Megan and I shared her story with the family, which led to a very uplifting praise and prayer service.

* * * * *

Throughout the summer, Megan continued to make miraculous progress with *zero* percent rejection and a *perfect* ejection fraction.

God's intent to continue to use Megan's miracle to bring people to Himself was becoming even more evident as Megan, Kathie, Wayne, and Sharon began getting calls to do interviews and speak at churches, retreats, and luncheons.

On June 8 Megan and her dad did a twelve-minute radio interview on KSIV in St. Louis. On July 13 Kay Quinn from Channel 5 KSDK went to the rehab facility to interview Megan during her workout. On July 14 Barnes released an updated story on Megan and televised her interview on July 19. The following week Megan told her story at her denomination's District Girls' Camp, meeting many of the girls who had prayed for her at the Bible Quiz on the day God gave the miracle. Megan spoke at her former youth pastor's church in Kansas. Sharon was scheduled to share Megan's miracle at a ladies' retreat, and Kathie would be the special speaker for a Christmas ladies' luncheon in Ohio. They weren't soliciting these opportunities; God was providing them.

Speaking to big groups wasn't what Megan considered to be her strength, but she was willing to let God lead her as she accepted the challenge to share her story.

In July, urged by her friends, Megan started her own blog site, "Come What May." As she wrote on the site she always felt, "Why does anyone care about reading my personal journal?"

On one special Sunday with her family, however, as they recapped the highlights of their experiences with Megan's heart, Megan realized that her blog did have a purpose. God wanted *her* to accept the challenge of telling *His story*.

Although Megan still felt inadequate and was afraid of public speaking, on that Sunday she promised God that she would even walk through the public speaking doors that He opened. She would accept all of the challenges that He gave. Megan was determined to face every challenge with her motto, "Through this I demonstrate that Christ is enough—come what may!"

When Megan first learned of her heart problem, way back in 2003, she'd written in her journal: "My dear God, please, please heal me. You know how much agony this sickness has put on my life and my family. Please give me back my healthy heart. Dear Jesus, if You heal me, I will give You all the praise and honor and glory. This will give me an awesome testimony to tell people that my God still works miracles today...and that a person can grow through trials and tribulations."

A few days later, she'd added: "Dear God, You are the God of miracles so touch my heart and heal it. Work a miracle in my life. Let my doctors see that it couldn't have been done with medicine but only through You! Let them see You through me. It will be an awesome testimony for me to tell how my God works. If you don't, I might not understand, but I will still be positive and love and trust You through it all."

Now Megan notes, "When I got home from my doctor's appointment on January 14, my sixteen-year-old heart was hurting and I really needed to talk with God. I grabbed my journal and began writing:

"Dear Jesus, I know You know I went to the doctor today. You know what the doctor said, and You know what I begged and prayed. Well, the outcome isn't what I wanted, but that means there are just bigger and better things for me out there. I will praise Your name even if it wasn't what I wanted. Take my life and take full control. I want what You want! Show me the bigger and better things You have for me. Bless me and enlarge my borders of witness for You."

"I now realize that I asked and God answered," Megan reflects. "Seven years later He pushed me to the brink of death so He would be the One to receive credit! He used me and is using me in ways I could not even have imagined. He worked in my life. He healed me! He's shown me the truth of 'Commit to the LORD whatever you do, and your plans will succeed' (Proverbs 16:3)."

Megan believes with all her heart that the God who chose her for this faith journey will walk with her through the rest of her earthly voyage, wherever it might lead. Faith has been successfully transferred to her, and her borders continue to enlarge as God continues His work in Megan's life and in Megan's heart.

* * * * *

"So each generation should set its hope anew on God not forgetting his glorious miracles and obeying His commands" (Psalm 78:7).

From Megan's Heart

Soon after Megan returned home with a new heart, friends began asking her to create a blog where she could tell about her experiences from her perspective. Megan reviewed some journals she had kept as a teen in high school, as well as the ones she had written in February and March before her transplant hospitalization. From that experience, the "Come What May" blog spot was created on Saturday, July 10, 2010.

Here's just a sampling from the pages of her blog.

* * * * *

Why me?

Now that I have a new heart, it is easy to look back and see what God had in store for me, but during those dark nights and long days of waiting during November 2009 through April 2010, it was tough. There were good days and bad days, emotional highs and lows, and thoughts of *what if?* I had days when my faith was incredibly strong and days when I cried myself to sleep.

After my bout with myocarditis when I was 15, doctors warned me I would be on meds for life and my heart would be damaged forever, but I didn't think it was that serious.

I still remember lying in the ER bed in November '09 when the doctor said I had severe congestive heart failure. I had been feeling sick but this had happened before and they always knew how to fix it. After being admitted to the hospital and releasing six pounds of fluid that had collected around my lungs, I felt like myself again.

By the time of my hospital stay a month later I was thinking, *Why me?* The nurse told me I was the youngest person in her ICU ward by more than 20 years. The next morning a boy my age was admitted. His heart was as bad as mine, but it was because of drug abuse. So, I again thought, *Why me? Why did I have to go through this when I've never done a drug? I am in here because I caught a virus that anyone could catch, young or old. I did not do anything to my body to deserve this.*

I quickly had to learn that God would not allow anything to happen to me that I could not handle. I finally began to feel thankful that God chose me to go through this. I know that this may sound weird, but I knew that God must trust me to let me go through something so serious. I was thankful that He chose to use me for a reason I did not know.

* * * * *

I'll never forget the night in the hospital when I was first put on the IV heart medicine. I felt horrible: very jittery and my heart was racing. The nurse quickly got the doctor. After he examined me, he asked my mom, "Does she look sick to you?"

Mom answered a quick, "Yes," with sadness and worry in her eyes. I will never forget that moment. I started to realize then that my condition was serious. The doctor placed me on a medicine that would help my heart pump better. The good news was: it worked. The bad news was: now I was dependent on it.

That night I continued to feel nauseated and jittery and couldn't fall asleep. I tossed and turned while watching my precious mom sleep in the uncomfortable recliner next to me. At the end of my prayer that night, I did something I'd never done before; I asked Jesus to just come down and spoon with me. I was already turned on my side, so why not just ask?

Within a few minutes, I was no longer jittery. I felt a complete calmness. I will never forget the night I fell asleep in the arms of Jesus.

* * * * *

It's February 8, 2010, and I am sitting here listening to music and thinking about everything that has happened. I never thought I would depend on a medicine to stay alive. This situation definitely makes me re-evaluate my life. *For what or who am I living? What am I doing to pass my time? Am I living my life to the fullest? Am I the person I want to be?*

The last couple of months have been difficult; however, I have had this unbelievable peace. I really feel everything is going to be okay, and when it is all over, I am going to come out stronger: physically, emotionally, and spiritually. I know that somehow, and in some way, God will receive the glory from this. I feel sometimes that I should be breaking down most nights, crying myself to sleep, but Jesus has given me strength.

I am embarrassed to admit that it took this huge trial to cause me to grow closer to Jesus, but it did. I *knew* everything before, but I really *feel* everything now. I have learned to pray and to enjoy it. Prayer used to seem difficult to me, but now I realize it is really just talking. You can say anything you want, and whenever you want, and even wherever you want. These days I often pray myself to sleep.

* * * * *

My days are getting tougher and so many questions continually come to mind. *Will I get a heart transplant? Will God heal my own heart? How long will I be waiting?* I know that only time will tell, and I must be patient, but it's difficult when I am longing to feel good again.

It is embarrassing to have someone come up and talk to you and not be able to say more than a few words back because of shortness of breath. I cry because I cannot belt out while singing along to my favorite songs. It is a strange feeling to be too weak to shower and not be able to wash my own hair.

It is difficult when friends want to come see me, but I can never give them a definite time because I never know how I am going to feel on that day. Am I going to lose my friends? Do they understand? When I get better, will I already be forgotten?

When I grapple with all of these discouraging questions, I remember that I am a child of God. That thought alone gives me great comfort. He is really trying to do something in my life right now, and I am *so* eager to see the outcome. He has brought John 1:12 to my mind several times lately; because I have believed and received Jesus as my Savior, I have the right to be called a child of God. I am *His child!*

So many nights I cannot sleep through the night. Just like a small baby wakes up in the night and cries for her mom or dad, I have also been waking up and crying for my Heavenly Father. "Show me, Father, teach me. Tell me what You want me to learn from this so it can all be over. Hold me, and comfort me."

Just like a mom and dad comforts the small baby, My Father comforts me. I am a child of God (John 1:12).

******

Life is so short. I realize that more now than ever. Since my transplant, I am so thankful for each breath I breathe, for each new day that I wake up, and especially for the little things in life.

I learned from Psalm 37:7 that Jesus wants me to sit quietly in His presence and wait patiently for Him. I know how difficult it is to be patient when you want answers right now. However, I learned that the answer God gives will not only be exactly what you need, but it will be perfectly timed. If you patiently trust Him, eventually you will be thankful that He answered your prayers the way He chose to.

Are you facing uncertainties and no-hope dilemmas in your life? Rest in the Lord. Sit quietly in His presence. Consciously calm your mind so you can be ready to receive what He wants to tell you. Do not worry about tomorrow. Walk with Jesus today, and let Him guide your steps. Communicate with Him, and let Him be your closest friend. Jesus wants to be your guide. Trust His path for your life, and let Him guide you all the way to heaven.

Life is short. Why not choose today to walk the rest of your steps in life with my best friend, Jesus?

To read Megan's full "Come What May" blog posts, go to: meganrmoss.blogspot.com.

To contact the author or schedule a presentation of Megan's Heart, visit www.megansheart.com.